Novel Thinking Lesson Guide

Shiloh

Novel Thinking Lesson Guides
Charlie and the Chocolate Factory
Charlotte's Web
Shiloh
In Their Own Words: Abraham Lincoln
George's Marvelous Medicine
Abraham Lincoln

Written By
Ryan P. Foley
Norman J. Larson

Graphic Design By
Danielle West
Trisha Dreyer
Annette Langenstein

Edited by
Stephanie Stevens
Patricia Gray

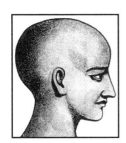

© 2008
THE CRITICAL THINKING CO.™
www.CriticalThinking.com
Phone: 800-458-4849 Fax: 831-393-3277
P.O. Box 1610 • Seaside • CA 93955-1610
ISBN 978-1-60144-177-5

ABOUT THE AUTHORS

Ryan P. Foley received his BA in elementary education from Loras College. He has been a fourth grade teacher since 2003. Mr. Foley has also taught special education students and has been a coach at summer camp.

Norman J. Larson received his BA in elementary education with a concentration in social studies from Clarke College. He has 15 post-graduate credit hours in the areas of literature and education. In 1999 he received National Board Certification as a Middle Childhood Generalist. He has been a teacher since 1994 and a fourth grade teacher since 1996.

The authors wrote these lesson guides after trying unsuccessfully to find existing quality materials for student use in order to teach novels effectively.

Table of Contents

About the Authors ii

Teaching Suggestions viii

Chapter 1 .... Pages 1-5
    Exercise A 1
- Vocabulary Development
- Parts of Speech

    Exercise B 1
- Context Clues

    Exercise C 2
- Characters

    Exercise D 3
- Setting

    Exercise E 3-5
- Inference
- Main Idea
- Details
- Cause and Effect
- Compare/Contrast

Chapter 2 .... Pages 6-10
    Exercise A 6
- Vocabulary Development
- Parts of Speech

    Exercise B 7-8
- Context

    Exercise C 7
- Characters

    Exercise D 8
- Inference
- Cause and Effect
- Drawing Conclusions
- Summarizing
- Details

    Exercise E 8-10
- Reading Comprehension
- Cause and Effect
- Inferences
- Main Idea and Supporting Details
- Problem and Solution
- Plot

Chapter 3 .... Pages 11-13
    Exercise A 11
- Vocabulary Development
- Parts of Speech

    Exercise B 11
- Synonyms

    Exercise C 12
- Characters

Exercise D 12-13
- Main Idea
- Cause and Effect
- Details
- Drawing Conclusions
- Compare/Contrast
- Inference

Chapter 4 .... Pages 14-16
Exercise A 14
- Vocabulary Development
- Parts of Speech
Exercise B 15
- Word Scramble
Exercise C 15-16
- Inference
- Prediction
- Details
- Cause and Effect
- Main Idea
- Sequencing

Chapter 5 .... Pages 17-19
Exercise A 17
- Vocabulary Development
- Parts of Speech
Exercise B 17
- Context
Exercise C 18-19
- Details
- Drawing Conclusions
- Sequencing
- Main Idea
- Cause and Effect
- Drawing Predictions

Chapter 6 .... Pages 20-23
Exercise A 20
- Vocabulary Development
- Parts of Speech
Exercise B 21
- Synonyms
Exercise C 21-23
- Main Idea
- Cause and Effect
- Details
- Sequencing
- Inference
- Main Idea
- Summarizing

Chapter 7 ....**Pages 24-28**

Exercise A 24
- Vocabulary Development
- Parts of Speech

Exercise B... 24
- Context Clues

Exercise C... 25
- Sequencing

Exercise D... 26
- Compare/Contrast

Exercise E... 26
- Setting

Exercise F...27-28
- Details
- Inference
- Compare/Contrast
- Drawing Conclusions
- Main Idea
- Sequencing
- Summarizing

Chapters 8 and 9...**Pages 29-33**

Exercise A 29
- Vocabulary Development
- Parts of Speech

Exercise B... 30
- Word Scramble

Exercise C..30-33
- Drawing Conclusions
- Cause and Effect
- Inference
- Details
- Main Idea
- Sequencing

Chapter 10...**Pages 34-39**

Exercise A 34
- Vocabulary Development
- Parts of Speech

Exercise B... 35
- Context Clues

Exercise C... 35
- Characters

Exercise D... 36
- Setting

Exercise E..36-37
- Main Idea and Supporting Details

Exercise F 37-39
- Summarizing
- Drawing Conclusions
- Details
- Cause and Effect
- Inference
- Compare/Contrast
- Main Idea

Chapter 11 .... Pages 40-43
Exercise A 40
- Vocabulary Development
- Parts of Speech
Exercise B 41
- Antonyms
Exercise C 41-43
- Cause and Effect
- Details
- Inference
- Summarizing
- Drawing Conclusions
- Making Predictions

Chapter 12 .... Pages 44-47
Exercise A 44
- Vocabulary Development
- Parts of Speech
Exercise B 45
- Which Word
Exercise C 45-47
- Compare/Contrast
- Details
- Main Idea
- Inference
- Summarizing
- Sequencing
- Details

Chapter 13 .... Pages 48-51
Exercise A 48
- Vocabulary Development
- Parts of Speech
Exercise B 49
- Context
Exercise C 49-51
- Details
- Drawing Conclusions
- Main Idea and Supporting Details
- Summarizing

Chapter 14 ....Pages 52-55
   Exercise A 52
     • Vocabulary Development
     • Parts of Speech
   Exercise B 52
     • Word Scramble
   Exercise C 53-55
     • Inference
     • Cause and Effect
     • Drawing Conclusions
     • Details
     • Main Idea

Chapter 15 ....Pages 56-63
   Exercise A 56
     • Vocabulary Development
   Exercise B 57-58
     • Context
     • Parts of Speech
   Exercise C 59
     • Which Word
   Exercise D 59-60
     • Characters
   Exercise E 60-63
     • Details
     • Inference
     • Drawing Conclusions
     • Sequencing
     • Main Idea
     • Drawing Conclusions

Compare/Contrast Writing Paper 64-69

Creative Story 70-75

Extension Activities 76-77

Answers 79-95

Teaching Suggestions

The *Novel Thinking* books are student-oriented lesson guides, aimed at enhancing both reading comprehension skills and vocabulary. The intent is to provide structured, pragmatic, and easy-to-use supplemental classroom materials based on novels of interest to a particular grade level.

These lesson guides include the following language arts skills in the comprehension questions:

- Main Idea and Supporting Details
- Characters, Setting, and Plot
- Problem and Solution
- Cause and Effect
- Making Inferences and Predictions
- Drawing Conclusions
- Comparing and Contrasting
- Cause and Effect
- Sequencing

Vocabulary skills such as context clues, synonyms, and naming parts of speech are emphasized. Writing activities that use compare/contrast and descriptive writing are also included.

Comprehension Exercises
Students are instructed to answer in complete sentences whenever possible.

Scoring Methodology
Comprehension
Each question has a possible total of 10 points.
- 5 points for content
- 5 points for grammar and punctuation

Students are awarded points based on the accuracy of their answers (content) and the format in which they provide the information (sentence structure). Setting a five-point range in each area allows the teacher to provide the student with an evaluation of student skills across a broader base.

All Other Sections
Each question is scored on content, and points are indicated following each question.

Name: _____ Date: _____

Chapter 1

A. Vocabulary: Write the underlined vocabulary word next to its definition below. Then name the part of speech (noun, verb, adverb, or adjective) for each word.

1. Marty didn't want to bite down on <u>**buckshot**</u>, so he checked each piece of rabbit.
2. Marty's favorite place to walk is just across the <u>**rattly**</u> bridge where the road curves by the old Shiloh schoolhouse and follows the river.
3. Something really hurts inside of you when you see a dog <u>**cringe**</u> like that.
4. Marty goes as far as the <u>**ford**</u>, where the river spills across the path.
5. Shiloh follows Marty across the bridge and then on past the <u>**gristmill**</u>.
6. Shiloh goes as far as the <u>**sycamore**</u> tree, lies down on the wet grass, head on his paws.

WORD	PART OF SPEECH	DEFINITION
a. _____	_____	to shrink from danger or fear; crouch in fear
b. _____	_____	a tall North American shade tree with bark that peels or breaks off
c. _____	_____	tiny balls of lead packed inside a shell casing; used to shoot wild game, such as rabbit
d. _____	_____	a place that grinds grain into flour
e. _____	_____	a place where a river or stream is not too deep to cross by walking or driving through it
f. _____	_____	making short sharp sounds; creaking

B. Context Clues: Write the correct vocabulary word to complete each sentence. Use each word just once.

1. The pioneers followed the river until they found a _____ to cross to the other side.
2. In the forest, among the _____ and evergreen trees, was a Chippewa village.
3. The hunter carefully cleaned out the _____ from the squirrel before cooking it.
4. The sight of the bear made the dog _____ in fear.
5. Farmer Jones took the wheat grain to the _____ to have it ground into flour.
6. The _____ car puffed and chugged up the mountainside.

C. Characters: Identify the characters introduced in Chapter 1. Then tell two things about each character.

1. Who is telling the story? _____

    _____

    _____

    _____

2. Who is Mrs. Preston? _____

    _____

    _____

    _____

3. Who asks if Dad shot the rabbit's head off? _____

    _____

    _____

    _____

4. Who is Mr. Preston? _____

    _____

    _____

    _____

5. Who else is at the table? _____

    _____

    _____

    _____

6. Who is 'Dog'? _____

    _____

    _____

    _____

D. **Setting**: The time (when) and location (where) in which a story takes place is called the setting. Using complete sentences, tell about the setting of *Shiloh*.

  1. When:

  _____

  _____

  2. Where:

  _____

  _____

  _____

E. **Comprehension**: Answer the following questions in your own words using complete sentences. Use supporting details from the book where applicable.

  1. a. Who was the narrator (the one who tells it) of this story? b. What in the book made you think that? Give 2 reasons.

  a. _____

  _____

  b. _____

  _____

  2. Ma was complaining when she said, "...see food go direct from the dish into somebody's mouth without a detour." What two actions was she referring to?

  _____

  _____

  3. a. Why didn't Marty eat the rabbit? b. What do you think was Marty's main concern about animals?

  a. _____

  _____

  b. _____

  _____

4. How did Shiloh act around Marty when they first met? Give two examples.

    _____

    _____

    _____

    _____

5. a. What did Marty do that changed Shiloh's reaction to him? b. What effect did
    it have on Shiloh? Give two examples.

    a. _____

    _____

    _____

    b. _____

    _____

    _____

6. A simile is when two unlike things are compared with something in common. What
    did Shiloh's tail have in common with a propeller?

    _____

    _____

    _____

    _____

7. What was on Marty's mind as he walked home with Shiloh following him? Give two
    things.

    _____

    _____

    _____

    _____

8. What made Marty tell Shiloh to go home when they reached his house? Give two reasons.

   _____

   _____

   _____

   _____

9. After his dad said he believed it was Judd Travers' new hunting dog, Marty gave some reasons why Shiloh shouldn't go back. Give two of his reasons.

   _____

   _____

   _____

   _____

10. a. Why did Marty name the dog Shiloh? b. What do you think it meant when Marty gave the dog a name?

   a. _____

   _____

   _____

   b. _____

   _____

   _____

Name: _____ Date: _____

Chapter 2

A. **Vocabulary:** Fill in the puzzle using the vocabulary words and the definitions below.

veterinary	mush	loping	flustered
mistreated	peering	coon	patience

Across

3. treated badly
5. made nervous and excited; confused
7. short for raccoon

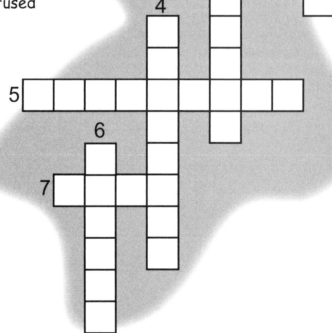

Down

1. looking closely to see clearly
2. of or about the medical treatment of animals
3. corn meal boiled in water or milk
4. willingness to put up with waiting
6. running with a long, easy stride

B. Context: Read each of the following sentences. Then use each underlined vocabulary word in a new sentence. Finally, name the part of speech (noun, verb, adverb, or adjective) for each vocabulary word.

1. If there are no leftovers, Ma takes cold cornmeal **_mush_**, fries up big slabs, and we eat it with Karo syrup.

   _____

   _____

   Part of Speech: _____

2. When Marty whistles softly, Shiloh comes **_loping_** toward him.

   _____

   _____

   Part of Speech: _____

3. To be a vet, you've got to have college training and it takes a lot of money to go to **_veterinary_** school.

   _____

   _____

   Part of Speech: _____

4. After Judd confused him, Mr. Wallace became so **_flustered_** he just dug in his money drawer and gave Judd change for a twenty.

   _____

   _____

   Part of Speech: _____

5. If this dog's **_mistreated_**, he's only about one out of fifty thousand animals that is.

   _____

   _____

   Part of Speech: _____

6. Judd's at the door of his trailer already, in his undershirt, **_peering_** out.

   _____

   _____

   Part of Speech: _____

7. Every time Judd takes that <u>**coon**</u> dog hunting, the dog runs off.

   _____

   _____

   Part of Speech: _____

8. That dog could be a fine hunting dog, but he tries Judd's <u>**patience**</u>.

   _____

   _____

   Part of Speech: _____

C. **Characters:** Identify the new characters who appeared in Chapter 2. Then tell two things about each character.

   1. Which character didn't Marty like? _____

      _____

      _____

   2. Who did Judd cheat out of money? _____

      _____

      _____

D. **Setting:** Marty and his dad traveled to a neighbor's place. Tell 2 details about this new setting.

   _____

   _____

   _____

   _____

E. **Comprehension:** Answer the following questions in your own words using complete sentences. Use supporting details from the book where applicable.

   1. Why was there a discussion about food during supper that evening?

      _____

      _____

2. What did Marty do about finding food for Shiloh?

   _____

   _____

   _____

3. a. Where did Marty and his dad go after supper? b. How do you think Marty felt about this?

   a. _____

   _____

   b. _____

   _____

4. Marty changed his goal from being a vet to being a veterinarian's assistant. Why? Give two reasons.

   _____

   _____

   _____

   _____

5. How did Judd cheat Mr. Wallace? Give 3 details in order.

   _____

   _____

   _____

   _____

6. What was the reason Shiloh began to shake?

   _____

   _____

   _____

7. What did Marty ask his dad that might help Shiloh?

    _____

    _____

    _____

    _____

8. Why didn't Marty's dad ask Judd about Shiloh right away? Give two reasons.

    _____

    _____

    _____

    _____

9. What did Judd do when Shiloh leaped out of the Jeep? Why?

    _____

    _____

    _____

    _____

10. a. What did Marty tell Judd he would do? b. Why?

    a. _____

    _____

    _____

    b. _____

    _____

    _____

Name: _____   Date: _____

Chapter 3

A. Vocabulary: Write the underlined vocabulary word next to its definition below. Then name the part of speech (noun, verb, adverb, or adjective) for each word.

1. In a **_froggy_** kind of voice that shows you aren't woke up, Marty asks his father a question.
2. Marty fixes Becky a bowl of Cheerios, puts her sneakers on, and brushes the **_snarls_** from her hair.
3. Ma lifts the big iron **_skillet_** to the stove top and lays some bacon in it.
4. Ma sits in the swing, **_shelling_** lima beans for the next day.
5. Next morning Dad gives Marty a **_nudge_** when he comes through to the kitchen, and he is up like a shot.
6. Judd has got a big old **_sickle_** and is cutting weeds along his side of the road.

WORD	PART OF SPEECH	DEFINITION
a. _____	_____	to push slightly to attract attention
b. _____	_____	a shallow cooking pan with a long handle
c. _____	_____	hoarse, like a frog's croak
d. _____	_____	a tool with a short curved blade on a handle; used to cut tall grass or grain
e. _____	_____	tangles in the hair
f. _____	_____	taking a nut or vegetable out of its shell or covering

B. Synonyms: Circle the word that is a synonym of each vocabulary word. A synonym is a word that means the same or almost the same as another.

Vocabulary Word	Choice 1	Choice 2
1. froggy	cloudy	cracking
2. snarls	twists	laughs
3. skillet	pan	craftsman
4. shelling	shucking	collecting
5. nudge	bump	candy
6. sickle	car	mower

C. Character: Who do you think is the most interesting character up to now? Explain why.

_____

_____

_____

_____

_____

D. Comprehension: Answer the following questions in your own words using complete sentences. Use supporting details from the book where applicable.

1.   All night Marty thought about Shiloh. a. What did Marty think he made Shiloh feel and why? b. What did Marty decide he must do about Shiloh?

   a.   _____

   _____

   b.   _____

   _____

2.   a. Where did Marty sleep? b. Why?

   a.   _____

   _____

   b.   _____

   _____

3.   a. How did Marty's dad offer to help Marty? Give the 2 ideas. b. Why wouldn't his dad pay him for taking care of his sisters?

   a.   _____

   _____

   b.   _____

   _____

4. Why do you think Marty might have been discouraged that day? Give 2 reasons.

    _____

    _____

5. a. Why did Marty like to go with his dad on his job? Give 2 details. b. What was his dad's job?

    a. _____

    _____

    b. _____

    _____

6. When Marty saw his sisters catching lightning bugs and putting them in jars, how did he compare it to Shiloh's life?

    _____

    _____

7. What showed that Marty's dad is well-liked on his job? Give 2 details.

    _____

    _____

8. a. How did Judd treat his dogs? b. Why did he treat them that way?

    a. _____

    _____

    b. _____

    _____

9. Did the author's descriptions of Judd make you have negative feelings about him? Give 3 examples.

    _____

    _____

    _____

Name: _____   Date: _____

Chapter 4

A. Vocabulary: Write the underlined vocabulary word next to its definition below. Then name the part of speech (noun, verb, adverb, or adjective) for each word.

1. Marty eats his peanut-butter-and-soda-cracker sandwiches with Dad at noon, plus the <u>*zucchini*</u> bread Mrs. Ellison had left in her mailbox for him.
2. The new game <u>*warden*</u> in the county is plenty tough.
3. Ma's old washing machine didn't work—only the <u>*wringer*</u> part works if you turn it by hand.
4. There are <u>*burrs*</u> and <u>*stickers*</u> on the path up the hill, and usually Marty wouldn't take it without sneakers.
5. Marty gets as far as the <u>*shadbush*</u> next to the pine, and then he sits down and hugs Shiloh.
6. "Now what?" Marty asks himself. The problem is looking him <u>*square*</u> in the face.
7. Marty goes back down to the shed again, and he gets the old rotten <u>*planks*</u> Dad took off the back steps.

WORD	PART OF SPEECH	DEFINITION
a. _____	_____	a machine that squeezes water from wet clothes
b. _____	_____	a dark green squash shaped like a cucumber
c. _____	_____	a rough, prickly husk surrounding seeds of fruits or plants
d. _____	_____	facing straight at
e. _____	_____	North American bushes related to roses
f. _____	_____	any official who enforces certain laws and regulations
g. _____	_____	long, flat pieces of sawed lumber thicker than boards
h. _____	_____	sharp-pointed tips on stems or leaves; thorns

B. Word Scramble: Use the clue to help you unscramble each vocabulary word.

_____ 1. ABDHHSSU This plant would give you shade on a hot day.

_____ 2. AKLNPS A carpenter would use these to build a house.

_____ 3. BRRSU These might stick to your clothes if you walk in the woods.

_____ 4. ADENRW This officer protects wild game.

_____ 5. CCHIINUZ You can make a yummy type of bread with this vegetable.

_____ 6. EGINRRW This is a machine that takes the water out of wet clothes.

_____ 7. AEQRSU This is a shape with four sides.

_____ 8. CEIKRSST It would hurt your feet if you stepped on these.

C. Comprehension: Answer the following questions in your own words using complete sentences. Use supporting details from the book where applicable.

1. a. What did Marty find by the ridge about a year ago? b. What did he think happened and why?

   a. _____

   _____

   b. _____

   _____

   _____

2. Marty's dad talks about the new game warden. a. Do you think this might be of importance further on in the story? b. Why or why not?

   a. _____

   _____

   b. _____

   _____

   _____

3. Before Marty could buy Shiloh, he faced two problems. Judd was one problem.
    a. Why might that have been? b. What was the second problem?

    a. _____

    _____

    b. _____

    _____

    _____

4. Why didn't the Prestons have extra money to keep a pet?

    _____

    _____

    _____

    _____

    _____

5. Marty heard a soft noise and found Shiloh. a. What two things did Marty know
    once he saw Shiloh? b. What thought did Marty have that showed how he felt
    about protecting Shiloh?

    a. _____

    _____

    b. _____

    _____

    _____

6. List, in order, how Marty made a pen to keep Shiloh a secret? Give 4 steps.

    _____

    _____

    _____

    _____

Name: _____   Date: _____

Chapter 5

A. Vocabulary: Write the underlined vocabulary word next to its definition below. Then name the part of speech (noun, verb, adverb, or adjective) for each word.

1. As soon as I'm in the pen, Shiloh's up almost shoulder high to lick my cheek, **_nuzzling_** my hands, my thigh.
2. I **_slump_** down in the grass to rest.
3. Gradually the kitchen **_clatter_** dies down.
4. He **_commences_** to slobber love all over me as well.

WORD	PART OF SPEECH	DEFINITION
a. _____	_____	to drop heavily; to slouch down
b. _____	_____	noisy chatter
c. _____	_____	poking or rubbing with the nose
d. _____	_____	begins; starts

B. Context: Use each vocabulary word in a sentence.

1. _____

   _____

   _____

2. _____

   _____

   _____

3. _____

   _____

   _____

4. _____

   _____

   _____

C. Comprehension: Answer the following questions in your own words using complete sentences. Use supporting details from the book where applicable.

1. Marty identifies three problems he faced since he met Shiloh. Name them, then write solved or unsolved.

   a. _____

   _____

   _____

   b. _____

   _____

   _____

   c. _____

   _____

   _____

2. Why did Marty continue to collect bottles and cans?

   _____

   _____

   _____

3. List 3 of the steps Marty took to get food for Shiloh.

   _____

   _____

   _____

4. a. Who was at the Prestons' house when Marty returned? b. What did he want?

   a. _____

   _____

   b. _____

   _____

5. a. What did Judd say he'd do to Shiloh once he finds him? b. Do you think he really would do those things to Shiloh? Give 2 examples you've read so far in the book that support your answer.

    a. _____

    _____

    b. _____

    _____

6. a. How did Mr. Preston feel about Judd's threats? b. What 2 things did he say that support how you believe he felt?

    a. _____

    _____

    b. _____

    _____

7. Judd asked Marty if he had seen Shiloh. a. What did Marty say that suggested he hadn't seen Shiloh? b. Did he tell a lie? Explain your answer.

    a. _____

    _____

    b. _____

    _____

8. Knowing everything that has happened in the story so far, do you think Judd will get Shiloh back? What makes you think this?

    _____

    _____

    _____

    _____

    _____

Name: _____   Date: _____

Chapter 6

A. Vocabulary: Write the underlined vocabulary word next to its definition below. Then name the part of speech (noun, verb, adverb, or adjective) for each word.

1. Nothing Marty had told Judd was an **outright** lie, but what Marty had kept inside himself made Judd think that Marty hadn't seen his dog at all.

2. Then Marty let Shiloh go, and they race and **tumble** and laugh and roll.

3. The rain stops, the sun comes out, and all those worms are **oozing** up through the wet mud.

4. Ma is coming out to throw some **mash** to the hens.

5. Just for **devilment**, Dara plunks herself down beside Marty in the swing and starts doing everything Marty does.

6. Before going down to see David, Marty **tended** to Shiloh first, taking him a fistful of scrambled eggs.

7. Marty has brought up some old **gunnysacks** from the shed for Shiloh to lie on.

8. Marty knows he doesn't have to take a ride unless he wants, but if Judd is already **suspicious** about him, not taking one would only make it worse.

9. Far back as Judd could remember, his Pa took the belt to him—big old **welts** on his back so raw he could hardly pull his shirt on.

	WORD	PART OF SPEECH	DEFINITION
a.	_____	_____	raised, swollen ridges or spots made on the skin
b.	_____	_____	complete; open and direct
c.	_____	_____	mischief; behavior that causes harm or trouble
d.	_____	_____	to roll or toss about
e.	_____	_____	cared for; looked after
f.	_____	_____	slowly leaking a thick liquid out of small openings
g.	_____	_____	bags made from a strong coarse fabric made from jute (a fiber made from tropical plants)
h.	_____	_____	a warm mixture of bran or meal and water for horses and other animals
i.	_____	_____	belief that something is wrong

B. Synonyms: Write the vocabulary word that is a synonym to the words listed in the chart.

Vocabulary Words:

outright	tumble	oozing	mash	suspicious
devilment		tended	welts	gunnysacks

Synonyms	Vocabulary Word
1. roll; somersault	
2. sores; rashes	
3. seeping	
4. fed, watered	
5. suspect	
6. sacks; bags	
7. complete; total	
8. meal; slop	
9. trouble; mischief	

C. Comprehension: Answer the following questions in your own words using complete sentences. Use supporting details from the book where applicable.

1. a. What happened several years earlier that got Marty thinking about lies?
    b. Give an example of what Marty meant that "you can lie not only by what you say, but by what you don't say."

    a. _____

    _____

    b. _____

    _____

2. a. What conflict did Marty have about taking the food from home? b. Why did he think it was okay?

   a. _____

   _____

   b. _____

   _____

3. a. Who was David Howard? b. Why didn't Marty want David to come for a visit?
    c. What was Marty's solution to the problem?

   a. _____

   _____

   b. _____

   _____

   c. _____

   _____

4. What devilment did Dara Lynn do? Give 3 things in order.

   _____

   _____

   _____

   _____

5. Marty started up the hill with Dara Lynn following. Why did he talk about a snake?

   _____

   _____

   _____

   _____

6. What happened as a result of Marty sneaking half his breakfast for Shiloh? Tell about 3 outcomes.

    _____

    _____

    _____

    _____

7. a. Why did Marty go into Friendly? b. How did he plan on getting there?

    a. _____

    _____

    b. _____

    _____

8. a. Who stops to give Marty a ride? b. Why didn't Marty want to ride with him?

    a. _____

    _____

    b. _____

    _____

9. A summary is a short version of something that has been said or written, containing only the main points. Write a summary telling about the ride Marty and Judd take to Friendly.

    _____

    _____

    _____

    _____

    _____

    _____

    _____

Name: _____ Date: _____

Chapter 7

A. Vocabulary: Write the underlined vocabulary word next to its definition below. Then name the part of speech (noun, verb, adverb, or adjective) for each word.

1. Downstairs there's a kitchen, a dining room with a fancy light hanging over the table, a **_parlor_**, and a side room.
2. Marty told his ma the Howards had a room just for company. It was the first time Marty ever saw **_envy_** in his ma.
3. Marty rings the Howards' doorbell that sounds like **_chimes_**.
4. The fishbowl had sand in it and a hermit crab, **_scurrying_** around with a shell on its back.
5. After the sandwich there's **_tapioca_** pudding and chocolate-covered graham crackers.
6. Mr. Wallace is sort of talking without looking at Marty, the way folks do when they don't want to **_embarrass_** you.

WORD	PART OF SPEECH	DEFINITION
a. _____ _____		a feeling of desire because another person has what you want; jealousy
b. _____ _____		to make uneasy and ashamed; to make self-conscious
c. _____ _____		a starchy food obtained from the root of the cassava plant (a tropical plant)
d. _____ _____		running quickly; hurrying
e. _____ _____		a room for receiving or entertaining guests; sitting room
f. _____ _____		a set of bells that make musical sounds when struck

B. Context: Substitute the correct word from the vocabulary list for each underlined word or words.

1. The child added milk to the **_custard_** she was making for dessert. _____
2. Our neighbors have a clock that **_rings_** on every hour. _____
3. Darrel liked to **_shame_** his big sister whenever he could. _____
4. "Please wait in the **_sitting room_** while I awaken my wife," he said. _____
5. They robbed the store, then were seen **_dashing_** behind shelves to hide when the police came. _____
6. My cousin felt a pang of **_jealousy_** when I was given a new car. _____

C. Sequence: List the lettered events from Chapter 7 in the order (sequence) they occur in the story.

a. Mrs. Howard notices the way Marty picks up every crumb and asks Marty if he would like another sandwich.

b. Marty and David get out the blocks and build a maze with walls on both sides and put Hermie in it.

c. David comes whooping downstairs, carrying a helicopter that flies when you pull a string.

d. Shiloh and Marty go on a good long run over the meadow.

e. When Marty gets home, Mrs. Preston is ironing and watching TV and Dara Lynn and Becky are out on the front swing.

f. David and Marty go upstairs to David's room and David says he has a new pet to show him.

g. Marty goes down the street to the corner store and asks Mr. Wallace if he has any old cheese or lunch meat he can sell Marty cheap.

h. Marty doesn't feel good about the lies he tells Dara Lynn, David, and his ma, but he doesn't feel exactly bad either.

i. Marty rings the doorbell that sounds like church chimes on the Howard house.

j. Marty sneaks off up the hill with the can and all the food he has with him.

k. Mrs. Howard sits down to eat with the boys and talks about grown-up things.

l. Marty and David sit on the back steps and eat Popsicles Mrs. Howard made out of pineapple juice.

m. Mr. Wallace talks without looking at Marty, the way folks do when they don't want to embarrass you.

n. Marty puts a rock in the bottom of the can, sets it in the stream, and puts the food in it.

o. Marty starts down the hill and halfway to the bottom, he meets Dara Lynn.

p. Marty tells Mrs. Howard he has to be home by late afternoon, then she asks him to stay for lunch.

q. After the sandwich, the boys have tapioca pudding and chocolate-covered graham crackers.

1st _____

2nd _____

3rd _____

4th _____

5th _____

6th _____

7th _____

8th _____

9th _____

10th _____

11th _____

12th _____

13th _____

14th _____

15th _____

16th _____

17th _____

D. **Compare/Contrast:** A Venn diagram uses circles to show similarities, differences, and what is alike. The overlapping piece in the middle is where things that are alike are written. Using information from Chapters 1-7, fill in the Venn diagram about Marty and David.

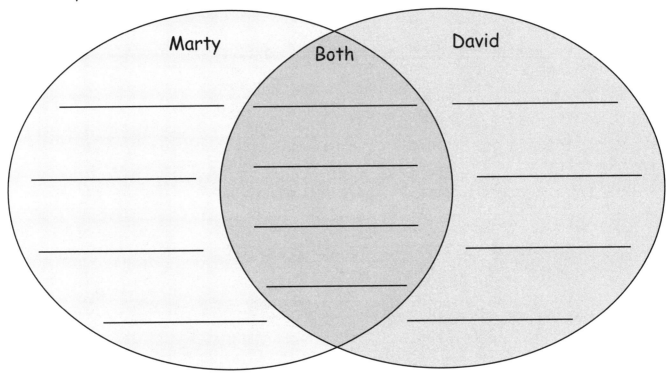

E. **Setting:** Give four details about the Howard house.

1. _____
   _____
   _____

2. _____
   _____
   _____

3. _____
   _____
   _____

4. _____
   _____

F. Comprehension: Answer the following questions in your own words using complete sentences. Use supporting details from the book where applicable.

1. a. What kind of pet did David Howard have? b. How did Marty feel about David's pet?

    a. _____

    _____

    b. _____

    _____

2. a. What lie did Marty tell David? b. Why?

    a. _____

    _____

    b. _____

    _____

3. Contrast the lunch Mrs. Howard served with what the boys usually had at Marty's house. Include 3 differences.

    _____

    _____

    _____

    _____

4. a. Why was Marty ashamed of himself? b. What did this tell you about his character?

    a. _____

    _____

    b. _____

    _____

5. a. What did Marty think about the lies he had been telling? b. Describe a situation where you might feel justified in telling a lie.

    a. _____

    _____

    b. _____

    _____

6. Marty doesn't go directly home from David's house. Where did he go and why?

    _____

    _____

    _____

    _____

7. a. What new problem did Marty have? b. How did he solve it? Give 5 steps in order.

    a. _____

    _____

    b. _____

    _____

    _____

    _____

8. a. What did Marty tell Dara Lynn when he found her coming up the hill and why?
    b. Marty didn't feel exactly bad about lying because of something Grandma Preston once told him. Explain what he thought about it.

    a. _____

    _____

    b. _____

    _____

Name: _____   **Date:** _____

Chapters 8 and 9

A. Vocabulary: Write the underlined vocabulary word next to its definition below. Then name the part of speech (noun, verb, adverb, or adjective) for each word.

1. Judd thinks maybe he could find some <u>*quail*</u> over in the far woods.
2. Marty takes Shiloh back to his pen, and Shiloh goes right to the gunnysacks in the lean-to, he's so <u>*tuckered*</u> out.
3. Dara Lynn wore her new sneakers home and got a <u>*blister*</u> already.
4. Marty puts away a wing and a thigh on a saucer and adds a spoonful of <u>*squash*</u>, which might be good for Shiloh's insides.
5. Seems like the sky's <u>*swirling*</u> around above Marty, with tree branches going every which way.
6. Ma <u>*crouches*</u> down in the soft pine needles, and Shiloh starts leaping up on her with his front paws.
7. When Marty leaps out of bed, he needs to <u>*thrust*</u> his feet into his sneakers before he races toward the back door.
8. Shiloh's got blood on his side, his ear, a big open <u>*gash*</u> on one leg, and he doesn't move.

WORD	PART OF SPEECH	DEFINITION
a. _____	_____	a vegetable that grows from trailing vines on the ground
b. _____	_____	any of various plump game birds belonging to the same family as the pheasant
c. _____	_____	a small swelling in the skin filled with watery liquid
d. _____	_____	tired; exhausted
e. _____	_____	a long, deep cut or wound
f. _____	_____	moving with a twisting, circling motion
g. _____	_____	to push with force
h. _____	_____	stoops low with bent legs

B. Word Scramble: Use the clue to help you unscramble each vocabulary word.

1. _____ CCEHORSU The way to get close to pet a small creature.

2. _____ GIILNRSW This is what the wind is doing in a tornado.

3. _____ AGHS What you might get if you are not careful with a sharp knife.

4. _____ HRSTTU How a knight might use his sword.

5. _____ UILAQ Something one might serve roasted for dinner.

6. _____ EEKRUDCT Exhausted; how you'd feel after shoveling dirt all day.

7. _____ SHQUAS These grow ripe on the ground.

8. _____ SREIBTL If you didn't wear gloves when shoveling dirt, you'll find these on your hands.

C. Comprehension: Answer the following questions in your own words using complete sentences. Use supporting details from the book where applicable.

1. a. What news did Marty find out at dinner? b. How did you know he was upset? Give 2 details. c. Why did the news upset him?

   a. _____

   _____

   b. _____

   _____

   c. _____

   _____

2. a. What couldn't Mr. Preston figure out when he finished his route? b. Tell why Marty figured he knew what was going on.

    a. _____

    _____

    b. _____

    _____

3. a. What happened while Ma was in town? Give 2 details. b. Who else do you think was responsible for people asking Ma how she's feeling? Why?

    _____

    _____

    _____

    _____

    _____

4. Describe Marty's and Shiloh's favorite game and what they do after.

    _____

    _____

    _____

    _____

5. a. What do you think made Mrs. Preston begin to suspect Marty might have Judd's dog? b. What did Mrs. Preston tell Marty was the final clue?

    a. _____

    _____

    b. _____

    _____

6. As she reached out and stroked Shiloh, she said, "We've got ourselves a secret."
    How did Marty feel about what she said?

    _____

    _____

    _____

    _____

    _____

7. a. Why did Marty's ma tell him it's important for her to tell his dad? b. Do you
    think they've ever lied to each other? c. What makes you think that?

    a. _____

    _____

    _____

    b. _____

    _____

    _____

    c. _____

    _____

    _____

8. What agreement did Marty and his ma make?

    _____

    _____

    _____

    _____

    _____

9. a. What did Marty plan to do with Shiloh? b. How would he be able to honestly say he didn't know where the dog was?

_____

_____

_____

_____

_____

10. What happened after the family heard Shiloh yelping? Include at least 12 actions, in order.

_____

_____

_____

_____

_____

_____

_____

_____

_____

_____

_____

Name: _____ Date: _____

Chapter 10

A. Vocabulary: Write the underlined vocabulary word next to its definition below. Then name the part of speech (noun, verb, adverb, or adjective) for each word.

1. Marty could see Shiloh <u>**wince**</u> and pull back on his leg where it hurts.
2. Doc Murphy puts on his <u>**stethoscope**</u> and listens to Shiloh's heart.
3. The thing to worry about now, with Shiloh's wounds, is <u>**infection**</u>.
4. Doc slowly inserts the needle in Shiloh's side, and Marty gets up the <u>**nerve**</u> to tell Doc whose dog Shiloh is.
5. Doc Murphy washes the wounds, <u>**dresses**</u> them, and starts stitching the skin back up.

	WORD	PART OF SPEECH	DEFINITION
a.	_____	_____	puts medicines and bandages on a wound or sore
b.	_____	_____	courage; mental strength
c.	_____	_____	a condition caused by germs entering the body, which can harm or destroy tissue
d.	_____	_____	a device commonly used by doctors to hear heart or lung sounds
e.	_____	_____	to draw back suddenly; flinch slightly

B. Context Clues: Write a vocabulary word to complete each sentence.

Vocabulary Words

wince	stethoscope	infection
nerve	dresses	

1. Because she didn't wash it with soap and water, Helga's cut had to be treated for

    an _____ .

2. Chi-Yun had to get up his _____ to tell that he had broken his father's fishing pole.

3. The pain made Katie _____ when she tried to walk on her sprained ankle.

4. After the nurse cleans the soldier's wounds, she _____ it with clean bandages.

5. The _____ felt cold when the doctor placed it on Travis' back to listen to his breathing.

C. Character: Name the character introduced in Chapter 10. Tell two things about this character.

_____

_____

_____

_____

D. Setting: Name the new setting introduced in this chapter and tell why it was introduced.

_____

_____

_____

_____

E. Events/Details: Listed below are some of the events that happen in Chapter 10. Give 3 supporting details for each.

1. Marty and Mr. Preston find the wounded Shiloh.

    a. _____

    _____

    _____

    b. _____

    _____

    _____

    c. _____

    _____

    _____

2. Doc Murphy helps Shiloh.

    a. _____

    _____

    b. _____

    _____

    c. _____

    _____

3. Mr. Preston and Marty talk after leaving Doc's house.

a. _____

_____

b. _____

_____

c. _____

_____

F. Comprehension: Answer the following questions in your own words using complete sentences. Use supporting details from the book where applicable.

1. Summarize what happens in Chapter 10. Remember that a summary is a shortened version of something, containing only the main points.

_____

_____

_____

_____

2. a. What do you think made Marty believe his dad was taking Shiloh back to Judd?
   b. Where was he really taking him?

a. _____

_____

b. _____

_____

3. Give an example of why the story says Doc Murphy had "a kind heart."

_____

_____

_____

_____

4.   a. What did Marty finally have the nerve to do? b. How did Doc Murphy react?

    a. _____

    _____

    b. _____

    _____

5.   a. What were the 2 things that Marty found hard to do? b. Why was each so difficult?

    a. _____

    _____

    b. _____

    _____

6.   Did Marty's father lose trust in him? Give 2 details to support your answer.

    _____

    _____

    _____

    _____

7.   Compare and contrast why Marty decided to take Judd's dog, and how his dad felt about it. Give 1 thing they have in common then 2 supporting points for each person's side of the situation.

    _____

    _____

    _____

    _____

    _____

    _____

    _____

8. What agreement did Marty and his dad come up with about Shiloh?

_____

_____

_____

_____

_____

_____

_____

_____

_____

_____

Name: _____   **Date:** _____

Chapter 11

A. Vocabulary: Write the underlined vocabulary word next to its definition below. Then name the part of speech (noun, verb, adverb, or adjective) for each word.

1. Marty can't go down to the doctor's office and start **pesterin'** Doc, with him having patients to see.

2. Marty asked David what he wants to do, trying to dig up the least little bit of **enthusiasm**.

3. David sees a groundhog, and the next thing you know he's after it--the groundhog **zigzagging** this way and that.

4. Marty goes over and has to **yank** David's arm to make him sit down.

5. Becky will probably **warble** the news about Shiloh to the first person coming up the lane.

6. Here's Doc Murphy's car **chugging** up the lane and he's got Shiloh with him in the back seat.

7. Doc thinks it is a **generous** thing to do when Marty tells him he will pay the bill for a dog that is not even his.

8. Doc got Shiloh sewn back up and full of **antibiotics**.

WORD	PART OF SPEECH	DEFINITION
a. _____	_____	to pull with a sudden motion; tug
b. _____	_____	a substance that destroys or weakens germs in an infection
c. _____	_____	eager interest
d. _____	_____	making dull bursts of sound as from a motor or engine
e. _____	_____	bothering; annoying
f. _____	_____	unselfish; willing to share with others
g. _____	_____	moving with short, sharp turns from one side to the other
h. _____	_____	slang for tattle or tell a secret

B. Antonyms: Circle the word that is an antonym to the vocabulary word. An antonym is a word that means the opposite of another word.

Vocabulary Word	Choice 1	Choice 2	Choice 3
1. pesterin'	bothering	helping	annoying
2. enthusiasm	boredom	excitement	zeal
3. zigzagging	swerving	veering	stopping
4. yank	push	pull	tug
5. warble	tattle	hide	gossip
6. chugging	sputtering	sound	noiseless
7. generous	selfish	giving	sharing
8. antibiotics	germicide	mold	robots

C. Comprehension: Answer the following questions in your own words using complete sentences. Use supporting details from the book where applicable.

1. "It's only after I lie back down on the couch that night that I realize what all I've done. To Ma and Dad, for one thing." These are the first two sentences in Chapter 11. How did Marty's actions affect his parents?

   _____

   _____

   _____

   _____

   _____

2. Tell how each of his sisters reacted to the news about Shiloh.

   _____

   _____

   _____

   _____

3. a. What did Marty think when his friend came to visit him? b. What 2 activities did one or both of them do?

   a. _____

   _____

   b. _____

   _____

   _____

4. Why did Marty suggest they make peanut butter-cracker sandwiches? Give 2 reasons.

   _____

   _____

   _____

   _____

5. How did each boy react when David finds Shiloh's pen? Give 4 reactions for each boy.

   _____

   _____

   _____

   _____

   _____

   _____

   _____

   _____

   _____

   _____

6.   What did they do together and how did it make Marty feel?

_____

_____

_____

_____

7.   a. What happened next that made everyone happy? b. What did Doc Murphy mean when he said he didn't know if he wanted his patients to see Shiloh?

a.   _____

_____

b.   _____

_____

8.   a. How did Marty plan to handle Doc Murphy's bill? List 3 steps in order.
     b. What did Doc Murphy say about Marty's plan?

a.   _____

_____

_____

b.   _____

_____

9.   Doc gave instructions about caring for Shiloh and the family was joyful to have the dog back. Predict where you think Shiloh will be kept and what his life will be like.

_____

_____

_____

_____

_____

Name: _____   **Date:** _____

Chapter 12

A. Vocabulary: Write the underlined vocabulary word next to its definition below. Then name the part of speech (noun, verb, adverb, or adjective) for each word.

1. Seems like Ma can't hardly pass Shiloh's box without reaching down to pet him, making low **_sympathy_** noises in her throat.
2. Becky shrieks every time she feels Shiloh's mouth **_slurp_** the crusts off her toast out of her fingers.
3. Dad takes a little dab of **_turpentine_** and rubs it on the tick's rear end, and the tick backs out of Shiloh's skin.
4. Marty's voice doesn't sound near as strong as his dad's—it's sort of **_quavery_**.
5. Travers **_squats_** down by the box, puts out his hand, and Shiloh leans away.
6. Marty and Dad know Judd's dog is missing. They take him in, and don't even have the **_decency_** to tell him.
7. Marty is **_figuring_** by the time Shiloh's better, everybody will love him so much they just won't let him go.

WORD	PART OF SPEECH	DEFINITION
a. _____	_____	eat or drink with a loud, sucking sound
b. _____	_____	crouches on the heels
c. _____	_____	shaky; trembly
d. _____	_____	act of sharing another's sorrow or trouble
e. _____	_____	proper behavior
f. _____	_____	thinking; considering
g. _____	_____	mixture of oil and resin obtained from various cone-bearing trees

B. Which Word: Use a vocabulary word to find out which word is described.

1. Which word tells about a liquid made from a pine tree? _____

2. Which word tells about a feeling? _____

3. Which word is a synonym of **thinking**? _____

4. Which word describes a way of sitting? _____

5. Which word tells how you might drink a milk shake? _____

6. Which word is an antonym of **steady**? _____

7. Which word tells the way you should behave? _____

C. Comprehension: Answer the following questions in your own words using complete sentences. Use supporting details from the book where applicable.

1. Compare your prediction at the end of Chapter 11 to how Shiloh ended up in Chapter 12?

    _____

    _____

    _____

    _____

2. a. At first, how did Mr. Preston act around Shiloh? b. What did Marty see his dad do later?

    _____

    _____

    _____

    _____

3. a. With Shiloh there in the house, what did Marty figure could happen? b. What was the trouble with his figuring?

_____

_____

_____

_____

4. What do you think Marty meant when he said, " It's like Shiloh's here and he's not—everybody's waiting for something to happen."

_____

_____

_____

_____

5. Give 4 details about the family and Shiloh over the next couple of days.

_____

_____

_____

_____

6. a .What had Marty been afraid would happen with 7 people knowing about Shiloh?
    b. How did Judd find out about Shiloh? Tell 3 of the steps in order.

    a. _____

    _____

    b. _____

    _____

    _____

    _____

7.   What did Judd say about the Prestons having his dog? Give 3 statements.

_____

_____

_____

_____

_____

_____

_____

_____

8.   a. What did Ma ask Judd? b. What was Judd's response?

a.   _____

_____

_____

_____

b.   _____

_____

_____

Name: _____ **Date:** _____

Chapter 13

A. Vocabulary: Write the underlined vocabulary word next to its definition below. Then name the part of speech (noun, verb, adverb, or adjective) for each word.

1. Marty wonders if they would send an ***investigator*** all the way out from Middlebourne to see about a man said to kick his dogs.
2. Uncle Clyde and Aunt Pat cannot take Shiloh because she's ***allergic*** to dogs, and he would make her sneeze.
3. The door's ***padlocked***, but it doesn't take much to get in, 'cause the top of the building's open where some of the roof's blown away.
4. Marty ***rehearsed*** his lines so often he can say them by heart.
5. Around here it's serious business when you got a ***quarrel*** with your neighbor and you got to carry it as far as the law.
6. When you live in hill country, it takes a while for the sun to rise because it has to ***scale*** the mountains first.

WORD	PART OF SPEECH	DEFINITION
a. _____	_____	practiced lines or movements that are to be said or done at a later time
b. _____	_____	a person who examines a situation closely
c. _____	_____	fastened with a portable lock that is opened with a key or a set of numbers or letters
d. _____	_____	a fight with words; an angry dispute
e. _____	_____	to climb up a steep place
f. _____	_____	having an unusual bodily reaction (wheezing, rash, hives) to certain things

B. Context: Use each vocabulary word in a sentence.

1. _____

   _____

2. _____

   _____

3. _____

   _____

4. _____

   _____

5. _____

   _____

6. _____

   _____

C. Comprehension: Answer the following questions in your own words using complete sentences. Use supporting details from the book where applicable.

1. Marty talked to his dad, Ma, and David about Shiloh and returning him to Judd. What did each of them tell him?

   a. Dad _____

   _____

   _____

   b. Ma _____

   _____

   _____

   c. David _____

   _____

   _____

2. a. What was Marty's next plan to hide Shiloh? b. Why did he decide it wouldn't work?

   a. _____

   _____

   b. _____

   _____

3. a. How did Ma and the girls feel about Shiloh? b. What 2 statements did they make that support your answer?

   a. _____

   _____

   b. _____

   _____

4. a. Where did Marty go on Sunday morning? b. What was he going to do there?

   a. _____

   _____

   b. _____

   _____

5. a. What offer was he going to make? b. What did he think might happen if Judd didn't agree?

   a. _____

   _____

   b. _____

   _____

6. What thoughts were worrying Marty when he was halfway through the woods?
    Give 4 of them.

    _____

    _____

    _____

    _____

    _____

    _____

7. a. What two animals did Marty see on the way, and where were they? b. Tell
    what happened to each of them.

    a. _____

    _____

    _____

    b. _____

    _____

    _____

Name: _____   Date: _____

Chapter 14

A. Vocabulary: Write the underlined vocabulary word next to its definition below. Then name the part of speech (noun, verb, adverb, or adjective) for each word.

1. He's wearing this army **_camouflage_** shirt, a brown cap, and the weirdest grin that could fit on a human face.
2. Judd Travers had gone out that morning with the clear **_intention_** of getting himself a deer.
3. He **_slogs_** over through waist-high weeds to where the doe lays.
4. It's on his dad's hunting **_regulation_** papers.

	WORD	PART OF SPEECH	DEFINITION
a.	_____	_____	plods or walks heavily
b.	_____	_____	a purpose; meaning to do something
c.	_____	_____	required by some rule or law
d.	_____	_____	cloth colored to help people blend in with nature

B. Word Scramble: Use the clue to help you unscramble each vocabulary word.

1. _____ GSLOS What a bear does to get to the river.

2. _____ MACFALEUOG What a hunter wears in the woods.

3. _____ GATOLEUNIR What rule athletes have to follow to compete.

4. _____ TINETINON What Jose had the best of.

C. Comprehension: Answer the following questions in your own words using complete sentences. Use supporting details from the book where applicable.

1. a. What adjective would describe Judd after he shot the deer? b. What in the story was a clue? c. What adjective would describe Judd after he saw Marty? d. What in the story was a clue?

   a. _____

   _____

   b. _____

   _____

   c. _____

   _____

   d. _____

   _____

2. Explain why Marty said, "Standing next to Judd, I feel taller than I really am."

   _____

   _____

   _____

   _____

3. a. Why was it wrong for Judd to shoot the deer? b. What would happen if the game warden found out? c. Why do you think it was especially bad to kill a doe?

   a. _____

   _____

   b. _____

   _____

   c. _____

   _____

4. a. Do you think Judd is really angry at Marty or himself? b. Why or why not?

    a. _____

    _____

    b. _____

    _____

5. a. Give 3 examples of Marty talking back to Judd—saying things that sounded
    braver than he was. b. Why do you think Marty was speaking that way to Judd?

    a. _____

    _____

    _____

    _____

    b. _____

    _____

6. a. What did Judd offer Marty if he helped him and didn't tell anyone about the
    deer? b. What did Marty want?

    a. _____

    _____

    _____

    b. _____

    _____

7. What deal did they both agree to concerning Shiloh?

    _____

    _____

    _____

    _____

8. a .Why was Marty happy about the deal? b. Why was Marty upset about the deal?

    a. _____

    _____

    b. _____

    _____

9. What did Marty want Judd to do, so he wouldn't go back on his word?

    _____

    _____

    _____

    _____

10. What were the three other things Marty worried Judd might do?

    _____

    _____

    _____

    _____

Name: _____   Date: _____

Chapter 15

A. Vocabulary: Fill in the puzzle using the vocabulary words and the definitions below.

definite	afford	sift	squaller
scooting	jubilation	rarin'	locust
wedge	legal	whetstone	kindling

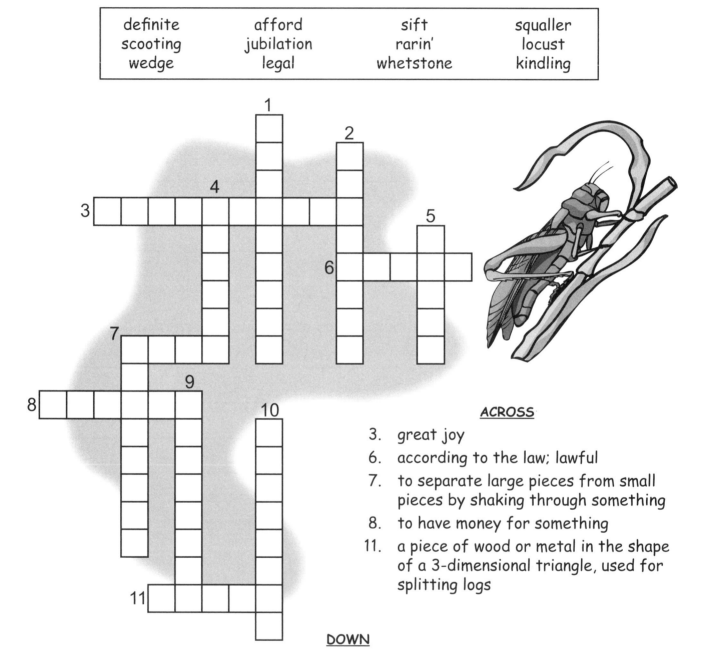

ACROSS

3. great joy
6. according to the law; lawful
7. to separate large pieces from small pieces by shaking through something
8. to have money for something
11. a piece of wood or metal in the shape of a 3-dimensional triangle, used for splitting logs

DOWN

1. stone used for sharpening knives or tools
2. small pieces of wood used to start a fire
4. a shade and lumber tree belonging to a group of several North American trees and bushes
5. very eager
7. moving quickly; darting
9. certain; without doubt
10. someone or something that will make a loud, harsh cry or noise

B. Context: Read each of the following sentences. Then use each underlined vocabulary word in a new sentence. Finally, name the part of speech (noun, verb, adverb, or adjective) for each vocabulary word.

1. Judd seemed pretty **_definite_** about keeping that dog.

   _____

   _____

   Part of Speech: _____

2. Now all the Prestons have to worry about is how they can **_afford_** to feed Shiloh as well as themselves.

   _____

   _____

   Part of Speech: _____

3. Judd wants the dirt chopped up so fine he can **_sift_** it through his fingers.

   _____

   _____

   Part of Speech: _____

4. Judd's biggest dog is the largest **_squaller_**. Judd can tell from the racket whether he's following a fresh track or an old one.

   _____

   _____

   Part of Speech: _____

5. After eating and talking to Marty, Dad was **_scooting_** back in his chair.

   _____

   _____

   Part of Speech: _____

6. Marty howls out in joy and **_jubilation_**.

   _____

   _____

   Part of Speech: _____

7. Judd's dogs were **_rarin'_** to go out rabbit hunting, pulling at their chains and snarling at each other.

_____

_____

Part of Speech: _____

8. Marty had to roll a big piece of **_locust_** wood over to the stump in Judd's side yard, drive a **_wedge_** in it, then hit the wedge with a sledgehammer.

_____

_____

_____

_____

Part of Speech: _____

Part of Speech: _____

9. Judd thinks Marty doesn't know what is **_legal_** and what's not since Marty signed the paper without a witness' signature.

_____

_____

Part of Speech: _____

10. The sickle was getting dull, so Marty got a **_whetstone_** to sharpen it for Judd.

_____

_____

Part of Speech: _____

11. Marty got the felling Judd's going to tell Marty he can take that paper he signed and use it for **_kindling_** to start a fire.

_____

_____

Part of Speech: _____

C. Which Word: Use a vocabulary word to find out which word is described.

1. Which word is an antonym of **unlawful?** _____

2. Which word has to do with money_____

3. Which word is to a dog, as shouter is to a man?_____

4. Which word is a synonym of **joy?**_____

5. Which word is a verb for a kind of enthusiasm?_____

6. Which word has rhymes beginning with "L" and "G"?_____

7. Which word names a tree? _____

8. Which word works with matches to make something new? _____

9. Which word means "for sure?" _____

10. Which word names a tool? _____

11. Which word tells how somebody is moving? _____

12. Which word sounds like a kind of rock? _____

D. Character: Describe how each of the characters below showed some personality or character change for the better in this chapter.

Marty: _____

_____

_____

_____

_____

Judd: _____

_____

_____

_____

_____

Mr. Preston: _____

_____

_____

_____

Shiloh: _____

_____

_____

_____

E. Comprehension: Answer the following questions in your own words using complete sentences. Use supporting details from the book where applicable.

1. How did Marty's parents react when they learned Judd would sell Shiloh to Marty?

   _____

   _____

   _____

   _____

2. a. When Marty was asked to explain why Judd changed his mind, what did he feel were his two choices in answering? b. Explain what 'lying by omission' means.

   a. _____

   _____

   b. _____

   _____

3. Marty's dad said there's food for the body, and food for the spirit. What did he mean when he said, "Shiloh feeds our spirit?"

   _____

   _____

   _____

   _____

4.   a. What caused Shiloh to bark? b. Why was it pitiful?

   a.   _____

   _____

   b.   _____

   _____

5.   Judd kept giving Marty harder and harder work. What did Marty think were the reasons?

   _____

   _____

   _____

6.   When Judd talked about his dogs, he said things Marty didn't know how to respond to. Give 2 examples.

   _____

   _____

   _____

7.   List in order the 10 tasks Judd gave Marty to do.

   1st _____

   2nd _____

   3rd _____

   4th _____

   5th _____

   6th _____

   7th _____

   8th _____

   9th _____

   10th _____

8.   a. What did Judd tell Marty that almost made Marty's heart stop cold? b. Why did Marty keep working? c. What did Marty tell Judd?

   a.   _____

   _____

   b.   _____

   _____

   c.   _____

   _____

9.   a. What two tasks did Marty do that Judd didn't ask him to? b. Why did he do them?

   a.   _____

   _____

   b.   _____

   _____

10.   What caused Judd to have a look of 'pure puzzlement' on his face?

   _____

   _____

   _____

   _____

11.   What made Marty decide to return to Judd's the next day?

   _____

   _____

   _____

   _____

12. a. What do Marty and Judd talk about on the 3rd day of the 2nd week? Give 2 details. b. How does Marty feel after Judd talks about his father?

a. _____

_____

_____

b. _____

_____

_____

13. At the end of the day of his last day of work, Judd gave Marty a collar for Shiloh. Why do you think he did this? Give two possible reasons.

_____

_____

_____

_____

_____

_____

_____

_____

_____

Name: _____　Date: _____

Compare/Contrast Writing Paper
Introduction

After reading Phyllis Reynolds Naylor's novel, *Shiloh*, watch the motion picture created from the book. While viewing the film, use a pencil and paper to take notes on any differences you notice between the book and the film.

Your notes will make it much easier to write your compare/contrast paper on the novel and the movie and enhance the quality of your writing project. Good, detailed notes smooth the transition to pre-writing and improve the overall quality of your paper. Use the novel and your movie notes to help complete the pre-writing sheet.

_____

_____

_____

_____

_____

_____

_____

_____

_____

_____

_____

_____

_____

_____

_____

_____

Name: _____ **Date:** _____

Compare/Contrast Pre-Write
Novel/Movie Event List

Novel 	Movie
Event	**Event**

Name: _____   Date: _____

Compare/Contrast 1ˢᵗ Draft Directions

Directions: Use a separate piece of paper to write 4 paragraphs using the instructions below. Do not use I, me, my, myself, our, we, you, your, or any other first or second person pronouns in your first 3 paragraphs.

Title: _____

Paragraph 1: Write an introduction stating what you are comparing and contrasting.
- a.   State the name of the novel and movie.
- b.   Get your audience interested in reading your paper.
- c.   3 or more sentences

Paragraph 2: Compare the similarities between the book and the movie.
- a.   Write a topic sentence about who or what are alike.
- b.   Give 3 or more details of events to support how they are alike.
- c.   4 or more sentences

Paragraph 3: Contrast the differences between the book and the movie.
- a.   Write a topic sentence about who or what are different.
- b.   Give 3 or more details to support how they are different.
- c.   4 or more sentences

Paragraph 4: Close the paper by bringing your ideas together.
- a.   Use at least 1 of the following conclusion strategies:
  - • Summarize the main points.
  - • Draw a conclusion about what you learned writing this paper.
  - • State whether you preferred the book or the movie and why.
- b.   2 or more sentences

Name: _____   Date: _____

Compare/Contrast Writing
Examples of Topic Sentences

Comparing

1. The novel and movie have many similarities.

2. The novel and movie are alike in many ways.

3. The novel and movie are the same in many ways.

4. The novel and movie resemble each other in many ways.

5. The novel and movie have a few similarities.

Contrasting

1. The novel and movie have many differences.

2. The novel and movie are unlike each other.

3. The novel and movie are opposite in many ways.

4. The novel and movie do not have many differences.

5. The novel and movie have few differences.

Name: _____   Date: _____

Compare/Contrast Writing
Editing (CUPS) 1st Draft

Directions: First, by yourself make all the necessary changes in red on your first draft. *Re-read each paragraph 4 times* checking for the following corrections:

1. **C**APITAL LETTERS
2. WORD **U**SAGE
3. **P**UNCTUATION
4. **S**PELLING

Next, have a partner give you suggestions and then, initial each part as you complete it together.

	Introduction Paragraph	**Comparing Paragraph**	**Contrasting Paragraph**	**Closing Paragraph**
"C"apital Letters	You	You	You	You
	Partner	Partner	Partner	Partner
Word "U"sage	You	You	You	You
	Partner	Partner	Partner	Partner
"P"unctuation	You	You	You	You
	Partner	Partner	Partner	Partner
"S"pelling	You	You	You	You
	Partner	Partner	Partner	Partner

Now write your final draft. Make sure to include your editing changes.

Name: _____   Date: _____

Compare/Contrast Paper Grade Sheet
Shiloh

(Put in the grading
scale used on progress
report card from the school.)
<u>Grading Scale</u>

_____ Plans and composes writing

_____ Revises writing   _____=_____

_____ Edits writing   _____=_____

_____ Communicates effectively using written language   _____=_____

_____ Applies spelling strategies to independent work   _____=_____

_____ Creates legible documents using cursive writing   _____=_____

Use the checklist below to help score the process writing project

_____ Did not use the pronouns *I, me, my, mine, myself, our, we, you, your,* or any
        other 1st or 2nd person pronouns in the 1st three paragraphs.
_____ Four paragraphs
1st Paragraph: Introductory Paragraph
_____ 3 sentences (at least)
_____ Introduce who or what you are going to compare and contrast.
_____ Get your audience interested in reading your paper.
_____ Give name of novel/movie.
2nd Paragraph: Comparing Paragraph
_____ 4 sentences (at least)
_____ Topic sentence about whom or what are alike.
_____ Supporting details: Tell how they are the same. (at least 3 events)
_____ Give details of events from the novel/movie.
3rd Paragraph: Contrasting Paragraph
_____ 4 sentences (at least)
_____ Topic sentence about whom or what are different.
_____ Supporting details: Tell how they are different. (at least 3 events)
_____ Give details of events from the novel/movie.
4th Paragraph: Closing Paragraph
_____ 2 sentences (at least)
_____ Students brought ideas together letting the readers know the paper is
        being concluded.
_____ Students used one of the strategies below (check which one).
        _____ 1. Summarize the main points.
        _____ 2. Draw a conclusion (what was learned writing the paper—do you
                prefer the novel or the movie?)
        _____ 3. Give your opinion on the novel/movie.

Name: _____   **Date:** _____

Creative Story: A man walking down the street is holding a frightened cat. He walks up to you and tells you that he saved the cat from its cruel owner who mistreated it. He says the owner is now after him for taking her cat. He puts the cat in your arms, but the cat still seems frightened. He asks you to help him save the cat by taking it home. He also wants you to give him a few dollars for gas so he can get out of town before the owner finds him. Use the story map to help gather information about your story.

Story Map

Characters:

Setting - Where:

When:

Problem facing the character(s):

Event(s) leading to the solving of the problem:

Solution to the problem:

Name: _____ Date: _____

Now use the information from the story map to write your creative story.
This will be your first draft.

Hints: Add a title to your story.
      Introduce the character(s).
      Tell about the setting.
      Develop the problem the character(s) must solve.
      Think about main events that will help solve the problem.
      Give some details about the main events.
      Have the character(s) solve the problem.

_____

_____

_____

_____

_____

_____

_____

_____

_____

_____

_____

_____

_____

_____

_____

_____

_____

_____

Name: _____   Date: _____

_____

_____

_____

_____

_____

_____

_____

_____

_____

_____

_____

_____

_____

_____

_____

_____

_____

_____

_____

_____

_____

_____

_____

Name: _____   Date: _____

Creative Story
Editing (CUPS) 1st Draft

Directions: First, make all the necessary changes in red on your first draft <u>by yourself</u>. ***Re-read each paragraph 4 times*** checking for the following corrections:

1. <u>C</u>APITAL LETTERS
2. WORD <u>U</u>SAGE
3. <u>P</u>UNCTUATION
4. <u>S</u>PELLING.

Next, have a partner give you suggestions and initial each part as you complete it together.

	Characters/ Setting Paragraph(s)	Problem Paragraph(s)	Main Events/ Details Paragraph(s)	Solution/ Ending Paragraph(s)
"C"apital Letters	You	You	You	You
	Partner	Partner	Partner	Partner
Word "U"sage	You	You	You	You
	Partner	Partner	Partner	Partner
"P"unctuation	You	You	You	You
	Partner	Partner	Partner	Partner
"S"pelling	You	You	You	You
	Partner	Partner	Partner	Partner

Now write your final draft. Make sure to include your editing changes.

Name: _____ Date: _____

Creative Story Checklist

_____Title

_____Characters are introduced.

_____Setting is described.

_____Problem is introduced.

_____Main events lead to the solution.

_____Details give more information about the main events.

_____Solution solves the problem.

_____Story comes to an end.

Name: _____   **Date:** _____

Creative Story Grade Sheet

Directions: Use the checklists below to help score the writing project.

_____ Plans and composes writing

_____ Revises writing

_____ Edits writing

_____ Communicates effectively using written language

_____ Applies spelling strategies to independent work

_____ Creates legible documents using cursive writing

_____ Title

_____ Characters are introduced.

_____ Setting is described.

_____ Problem is introduced.

_____ Main events lead to the solution.

_____ Details give more information about the main events.

_____ Solution solves the problem.

_____ Story comes to an end.

(Put in the grading scale used on progress report card from your school.)

<u>Grading Scale</u>

_____=_____

_____=_____

_____=_____

_____=_____

_____=_____

Name: _____ Date: _____

Extension Activity 1

What was your favorite part of the book? Why? Draw a picture of
the event and write a description (caption) below it.

_____

_____

_____

_____

Name: _____   Date: _____

Extension Activitiy 2

Story Study Questions: Use a separate sheet of paper to answer these questions using complete sentences in paragraph form.

1. The book is about a dog named Shiloh which is the title, also. If you had to re-title the book basing it on what the book is about, what two titles might you suggest? Remember not to tell the ending in the title.

2. What would you have done differently if you had been Marty? Give at least two examples.

3. Do you think the story would have been very different if a girl had been in the role of Marty? Give at least 3 details of why or why not.

4. Write about the following questions:
   a. Do you think you would have told untruths to protect Shiloh? When do you think telling a lie is acceptable?

   b. What do you think about a lie of omission?

5. Name one other animal that could have been substituted for the dog, Shiloh. Why do you think that animal might work out as the character in the story? What might be a major problem with using this animal rather than a small dog?

6. There were a few 'turning points' in the story where events could go one or two different ways. Give two of these and briefly tell how the story would have been changed.

7. Have you or anyone you knew ever had a similar experience of helping or taking in an animal? If so, tell about it. If not, describe what one might have been.

8. The author made readers feel (rather than just know) things about the characters. For example, when Shiloh first followed Marty home, the author made readers feel sympathetic for Shiloh by describing how he walked and stopped and didn't make a sound, then came when Marty whistled. Describe 2 other events in the story, giving details explaining what the author wrote to make the reader feel what he wanted the reader to feel.

9. There is at least one moral or lesson for readers to learn in the story. Give one.

10. If the book were longer, what continuing or future events do you think might happen? Predict how the ending might be different.

ANSWERS

Note: The wording of the students' sentences will vary but should include the information (detail).

Chapter 1

Page 1 A

Word	Part of Speech
a. cringe	verb
b. sycamore	noun
c. buckshot	noun
d. gristmill	noun
e. ford	noun
f. rattly	adjective

Page 1 B

1. ford
2. sycamore
3. buckshot
4. cringe
5. gristmill
6. rattly

Page 2 C

These characters must be listed in order. Traits or facts may vary.

1. Marty – 11 years old, March birthday, boy, son, brother, kind, shot gun but not at living things, cared about animals
2. Ma – wanted her kids to eat slowly, cooks big Sunday suppers
3. Dara Lynn – one of Marty's sisters, said what she thinks, dips her bread
4. Mr. (Ray) Preston/Dad - shot animals for food, gave Marty a .22 on his 11th birthday
5. Becky - Marty's other sister, eats fast
6. Shiloh - shorthaired beagle, white with brown spots, nervous, follows Marty, comes when you whistle

Page 3 D

1. When:
   - The story takes place in the present.
   - All the verbs are present tense.
   Where:
   - It took place in the country.
   - They could shoot things there.
   - They lived high in the hills above Friendly.
   - Wild animals lived around them.
   - The towns are Sistersville, Wheeling, and Parkersburg.
   - These towns are in West Virginia.

Page 3 E

1. a. A person named Marty Preston is the narrator.
   b. • His mother called him 'Marty.'
       • He called himself 'I' in the story.
2. Students need these 2 answers.
   - Dara Lynn dipped bread in cold tea.
   - Becky's beans were pushed off her plate.
3. Students need 1 of these answers.
   a. • He didn't like that it was shot in the neck.
       • He couldn't eat it after hearing it probably didn't die quickly.
   b. He didn't want animals to suffer.
4. Students need 2 of these answers.
   - Shiloh followed Marty at a distance.
   - He stopped when Marty stopped.
   - He backed off when Marty was close to him.
   - He was completely quiet.

5. a. Marty whistled.
    b. Students need 2 of these
       answers.
       · Shiloh barreled toward Marty.
       · He licked his fingers.
       · He jumped up against Marty's
         leg.
       · Shiloh made little yelps.
6. Shiloh's tail went like a propeller,
    round and round in a circle.
7. Students need 2 of these answers.
    · He wondered if somebody would
      come out and whistle for Shiloh.
    · He worried that he'd be in trouble
      when he arrived home wet.
    · He hoped Shiloh would turn
      around and go back.
8. Students need 2 of these answers.
    · They weren't allowed to have
      pets.
    · He knew they couldn't afford to
      feed Shiloh.
    · They didn't have money for a vet
      if Shiloh got sick.
9. Students need 2 of these answers.
    · He said that Judd didn't treat
      Shiloh right.
    · The dog was too scared to pee.
    · You don't have to mark a dog to
      hurt him.
10. a. The dog's name came from the
       place where Marty found him: the
       old Shiloh schoolhouse
    b. When he named the dog, it meant
       he cared about it and didn't want
       it to be mistreated any more. He
       probably wanted to keep it, but
       knew they couldn't afford a dog.

Chapter 2

Page 6 A

Across	Down
3. mistreated	1. peering
5. flustered	2. veterinary
7. coon	3. mush
	4. patience
	6. loping

Page 7 B
Sentences will vary.
1. noun
2. verb
3. adjective
4. verb
5. verb
6. verb
7. noun
8. noun

Page 8 C
These characters must be listed. Traits or
facts may vary.
1. Judd Travers – dishonest, mean, spits
   tobacco, mistreats animals
2. Mr. Wallace –honest, neighborly, does
   what's right

Page 8 D
Students need 2 of these answers.
· Judd's home was a trailer.
· Other dogs on the property were
  barking.
· The yard was muddy.
· There were boards laid out instead of
  a sidewalk.
· A porch was built on the side of the
  trailer.

Pages 8-10 E

1. Marty wanted to save some rabbit meat to feed Shiloh and Ma said he couldn't.
2. He went to the henhouse, broke an egg, and fed it to Shiloh.
3. a. They drove Shiloh back to Judd.
   b. Answers will vary. Possible answers are listed.
      - Marty felt sad about not keeping Shiloh.
      - He was upset about taking Shiloh where he would likely be hurt again.
4. a. Students need 2 of these answers.
      - Marty wouldn't need as long a time in training.
      - It wouldn't cost as much.
      - He knew his family didn't have a lot of money.
5. Students need 3 of these answers in order.
   - Judd gives Mr. Wallace a ten-dollar bill.
   - He talks to Mr. Wallace.
   - Judd tells Mr. Wallace that he gave him a twenty-dollar bill.
   - Mr. Wallace becomes confused (and/or flustered).
   - Mr. Wallace finally gives Judd change for a twenty.
6. They are approaching Judd's place, and Shiloh is afraid to go there.
7. Marty asked about reporting Judd for mistreating his dogs.
8. Students need 2 of these answers.
   - In the hills, you don't get down to business right away.
   - You say your howdys.
   - You talk about anything other than the real reason you came.
   - When the mosquitoes begin to bite, you say what's on your mind.

9. - He kicks Shiloh.
   - He's mad that Shiloh had wandered off again.
10. a. Students need 1 of these answers.
      - Marty will keep an eye out for Shiloh.
      - If Marty sees him, he will bring him back.
    b. Marty doesn't want Judd to kick Shiloh anymore.

Chapter 3

Page 11 A

Word	Part of Speech
a. nudge	verb
b. skillet	noun
c. froggy	adjective
d. sickle	noun
e. snarls	noun
f. shelling	verb

Page 11 B

1. cracking
2. twists
3. pan
4. shucking
5. bump
6. mower

Page 12 C

Answers will vary.

Page 12-13 D

1. a. Wording will vary.
   He felt Shiloh was disappointed in him because he gave Shiloh hope, but then returned him to Judd.
   b. Marty decided he has to buy Shiloh from Judd.

2. a. Marty slept on the couch.
    b. There were probably not enough bedrooms for everyone.
3. a. • His dad suggests he collect bottles and cans for recycling money.
        • He says he'll ask about jobs along his mail route.
    b. His dad believes that, "If you live in the house, you do your share like the rest of us."
4. • He walks 5 miles for just 7 cans and 1 bottle.
    • His dad hasn't found anyone who has a job for Marty.
5. a. Students need 2 of these answers.
        • He gets a soft drink at the gas station.
        • He likes to ride in the Jeep over the back roads.
        • He can pick up cans and bottles along the way.
    b. His dad is a mailman.
6. Answers may vary in comparing the two.
    He sees them putting the bugs in jars as making them prisoners, just as he sees Shiloh chained up as a prisoner.
7. Students need 2 of these answers.
    • Marty's dad knows everybody's name.
    • He always takes time to say something to them.
    • People sometimes leave him treats in their mailboxes.
8. Answers will vary.
    a. Judd treats his dogs:
        • Poorly, badly.
        • In a mean way.
        • Abusively.
    b. Judd keeps his dogs half starved, so they'll hunt, and be scared of him so they'll obey.

9. Students need 3 of these answers.
    • Judd stinks with mean sweat.
    • He doesn't shave very often.
    • He has tight, little eyes beneath bushy eyebrows.
    • His teeth are dark from tobacco juice.
    • The fat on his belly shakes when he laughs.

Chapter 4

Page 14 A

Word	Part of Speech
a. wringer	noun
b. zucchini	noun
c. burrs	noun
d. square	adverb
e. shadbush	noun
f. warden	noun
g. planks	noun
h. stickers	noun

Page 15 B
1. shadbush
2. planks
3. burrs
4. warden
5. zucchini
6. wringer
7. square
8. stickers

Pages 15-16 C
1. a. He found a dead dog (beagle).
    b. • He thought Judd shot it on purpose.
        • It wasn't a good hunting dog.
2. a. Answer will likely be "yes."

b. Wording of answer will vary. The game warden or sheriff might arrest Judd and then he couldn't hurt the dogs any more.
3. a. Judd might not sell Shiloh to Marty.
   b. He doesn't have the money to feed and pay vet bills for a dog.
4. The Prestons are poor because every spare cent the family has goes to help pay for nurses for Marty's grandma.
5. a. • Judd took the dogs hunting and Shiloh ran away.
      • Marty is not taking him back. Not now, not ever.
   b. Judd would have to shoot Marty before he would let Judd near Shiloh.
6. Students need 4 answers in order.
   • Got fencing and wire from the shed.
   • Wrapped it around 3 trees & fastened it.
   • Got planks from the shed.
   • Picked up an old pie tin for Shiloh's water.
   • Built a lean-to to protect Shiloh from rain.

Chapter 5

Page 17 A

Word	Part of Speech
a. slump	verb
b. clatter	noun
c. nuzzling	verb
d. commences	verb

Page 17 B
Sentences will vary.

Page 18 C
1. a. Where to keep Shiloh hid?
      solved
   b. Would Shiloh be quiet?
      solved
   c. How to secretly feed Shiloh twice a day?
      unsolved
2. He needed money to buy meat and bones from the grocer.
3. Students need 3 steps in order.
   • Marty said he gets full fast at dinner.
   • Then, he gets hungry before he goes to bed.
   • He said he gets hungry for meat and potatoes, not cornflakes.
   • He saved some food on a plate.
   • He put it in the fridge.
   • He told his sister not to touch it.
4. a. Judd Travers was at the Prestons' house.
   b. He wanted to find Shiloh.
5. a. Judd said he'll break Shiloh's legs whup him good, and starve him lean.
   b. Yes
   Students need 2 of these answers.
   • He kicked Shiloh.
   • He didn't feed him the night the Prestons first brought the dog back.
   • He tied him up where he saw the dogs eating.
6. a. He felt that what Judd was going to do was wrong.
   b. • He told Judd a dog with 4 broke legs would be no good.
      • When Judd mentioned shooting a dog, Mr. Preston told him the sheriff would get on him.

7. Wording of answers will vary.
   a. Marty told Judd he hadn't seen Shiloh "anywhere in our yard."
   b. It was a lie because Marty had seen Shiloh, but somewhere else.
8. Answers will vary.

Chapter 6

Page 20 A

Word	Part of Speech
a. welts	noun
b. outright	adjective
c. devilment	noun
d. tumble	verb
e. tended	verb
f. oozing	verb
g. gunnysacks	noun
h. mash	noun
i. suspicious	adjective

Page 21 B
1. tumble
2. welts
3. oozing
4. tended
5. suspicious
6. gunnysacks
7. outright
8. mash
9. devilment

Pages 21-23 C
1. a. He bit off the ear of Dara Lynn's chocolate rabbit.
   b. Answers will vary.
2. a. Food not eaten by him would be eaten at another time, which would save spending money for more food.
   b. It's his share of the food and he can do what he wants with it.

3. a. David Howard was a friend of Marty's who returned from vacation.
   b. Marty was afraid David would find out about Shiloh.
   c. Marty told his parents he will go to David's house and visit him there.
4. a. Students need 3 of these answers in order.
   • Dara Lynn started copying everything Marty did.
   • She sat in the swing like Marty.
   • When he sighed, she sighed.
   • He rested his arms on his head, so did she.
   • When he goes down off the porch, she does, too.
   • She starts to follow him up the hill.
5. Dara Lynn is afraid of snakes, so she quits following him up to Shiloh's pen.
6. Students need these 3 answers.
   • Shiloh isn't getting enough to eat.
   • Marty isn't, either and he's hungry.
   • Marty's so hungry he eats wormy peaches.
7. a. Marty's going to visit David Howard, who lives there.
   b. He's going to walk.
8. a. Judd Travers
   b. He didn't want to ride with him because he didn't like Judd and he was hiding Judd's dog.
9. Students' summary should include most of these points.
   • Judd asked if Marty has seen Judd's dog. Says it's too shy to stick to the roads.
   • Marty wanted to know how much Judd paid for Shiloh.
   • Marty said that you need to treat a dog good to keep him home then compares it to a kid.

- Judd told he was "whipped" by his father but didn't run off.
- Judd didn't want anybody feeling sorry for him.
- As Marty walked off, Judd said that he taught Shiloh to come to a whistle for food. Also, how he would "kick (Shiloh) clear to China" if he did something Judd didn't like.
- Judd told Marty to catch Shiloh and Judd would pick him up.

Chapter 7

Page 24 A

Word	Part of Speech
a. envy	noun
b. embarrass	verb
c. tapioca	noun
d. scurrying	verb
e. parlor	noun
f. chimes	noun

Page 24 B

1. tapioca
2. chimes
3. embarrass
4. parlor
5. scurrying
6. envy

Page 25 C

1st	i	10th	g
2nd	c	11th	m
3rd	l	12th	e
4th	f	13th	j
5th	b	14th	n
6th	p	15th	d
7th	k	16th	o
8th	a	17th	h
9th	q		

Page 26 D

Answers will vary.

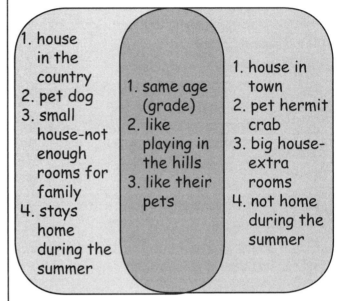

1. house in the country
2. pet dog
3. small house-not enough rooms for family
4. stays home during the summer

1. same age (grade)
2. like playing in the hills
3. like their pets

1. house in town
2. pet hermit crab
3. big house-extra rooms
4. not home during the summer

Page 26 E

Students need 4 of these answers.
The Howard house had:
- Two floors (3 counting the basement, 4 counting the attic).
- A big kitchen.
- 4 bedrooms (one spare, one for his dad's books and computer).
- A dining room with a fancy light hanging over the table.
- A parlor.
- A side room with a lot of windows just for plants.
- A porch that ran along 3 sides of the house.
- Once was owned by David's grandfather.

Pages 27-28 F

1. a. David had a hermit crab for a pet.
   b. Marty guessed any pet was okay, but he wouldn't trade Shiloh for all the hermit crabs in the world.

2. a. Marty said his ma has a headache and can't take any noise at all.

    b. Marty didn't want David to come to his house, because David might see Shiloh.

3. Mrs. Howard's lunch:
    - Had placemats under each plate.
    - Sandwich was filled with good things and a toothpick stuck in it to hold it together.
    - Included her as she ate and talked with the boys.
    - Had two desserts.

    Mrs. Preston's lunch:
    - Was packed for the boys.
    - The boys ate in the woods.
    - Left the boys on their own without her.

4. a. Marty ate all the food Mrs. Howard served him and didn't save any for Shiloh.

    b. Answers will vary.
        Marty felt responsible for Shiloh; for giving him all the food he could save from his own meals.

5. a. Marty felt that a lie doesn't seem like a lie when it's meant to save a dog.

    b. Answers will vary.

6. - Marty went to Mr. Wallace's corner grocery store.
    - He had 53 cents and asked to buy some old cheese or lunch meat for Shiloh.

7. a. Marty had to keep the food he bought from spoiling in the July heat.

    b. Students need 5 of these answers in order.
        - Marty found a can.
        - He put a rock in the bottom of the can to hold it down.
        - He set it in the cool stream and surrounded it with rocks.
        - He put the food into the can (sour cream, frankfurters, cheese, cookies).
        - He put the plastic lid on the can.
        - He set a large rock on top to keep the raccoons out.

8. a. Marty told about all the snakes on the hill to keep her away from Shiloh's pen.

    b. His grandma said there was a heaven and a hell, and liars go to hell. That's where he guessed he's headed. She also said only people go to heaven. Marty figured if that were true, he wouldn't want to be up there looking down at Shiloh left below anyway. So, he didn't feel all that bad about lying.

Chapters 8 and 9

Page 29 A

Word	Part of Speech
a. squash	noun
b. quail	noun
c. blister	noun
d. tuckered	verb
e. gash	noun
f. swirling	verb
g. thrust	verb
h. crouches	verb

Page 30 B

1. crouches
2. swirling
3. gash
4. thrust
5. quail
6. tuckered
7. squash
8. blister

Pages 30-33 C

1. a. Mr. Preston tells the family Judd wants to hunt quail on their land.
   b. Students need 2 of these answers.
      When Marty hears the news:
      - His whole body goes cold.
      - He wants to jump and scream.
      - He grips his chair.
   c. Maybe Judd suspected Marty was hiding Shiloh and was looking for an excuse to snoop around.

2. a. Mr. Preston doesn't know why more people are leaving food for him in their mailboxes.
   b. Mr. Wallace figured the Prestons were having money problems because Marty was buying old food. Mr. Wallace had told other people, who were leaving food to help the Prestons.

3. a. • Everything she bought was on sale.
      • People asked her if she was okay and told her what to take for headaches.
   b. Mrs. Howard, since Marty told her Ma was having headaches so David couldn't come up to his house.

4. Marty laid down on his back, covered his face with his arms. Shiloh used his nose to try to uncover Marty's face. When Marty took his arms away from his face, Shiloh rested his paws on Marty's chest. They both laid there all happy.

5. a. Marty had been keeping food from his dinner.
   b. When he asked for more of the squash he didn't like, she figured he was giving it to someone or something to eat.

6. He felt "some better" that the secret was now shared. He was tired of lying and keeping the secret to himself.

7. a. Mrs. and Mr. Preston hadn't kept secrets from each other in 14 years. If she did now, she didn't think he would ever trust her again.
   b. Answer will likely be "No."
   c. Explanation will vary.
      If they had lied to each other, they wouldn't have the trust that they still had.

8. • Mrs. Preston won't tell Mr. Preston for one day.
   • Marty promises not to run away.

9. a. He planned to give Shiloh away to someone driving through.
   b. He wouldn't ask where they were from so he could honestly say he didn't know where Shiloh was.

10. Students should include 12 of these answers in order.
   • Marty leaps out of bed.
   • He thrusts on his sneakers.
   • His dad says to get a flashlight.
   • Marty's already running up the hill.
   • Mr. Preston grabs a flashlight and follows him.
   • He shines the flashlight beam into the pen.
   • They see the German shepherd hunched over Shiloh.
   • There's blood on the shepherd's mouth and jaws.
   • The shepherd jumps out of the pen when Mr. Preston moves toward it.
   • Marty unfastens the pen and goes inside.
   • He kneels by Shiloh.
   • Shiloh has blood on his side, his ear, a big gash on one leg, and he doesn't move.
   • Marty puts his forehead against the dog, his hand on Shiloh's head.
   • He feels the dog's body shiver.

- Shiloh's tongue tries to move out to lick Marty's hand
- Marty's bawling and doesn't even care.

Chapter 10

Page 34 A

Word	Part of Speech
a. dresses	verb
b. nerve	noun
c. infection	noun
d. stethoscope	noun
e. wince	verb

Page 35 B

1. infection
2. nerve
3. wince
4. dresses
5. stethoscope

Page 35 C

Doc Murphy-short, kind, round belly, not a vet

Page 36 D

- The new setting is Doc Murphy's house.
- That is where Mr. Preston and Marty took Shiloh to fix his wounds.

Pages 36-37 E

Answers will vary. Examples are listed below.

1. a. Mr. Preston held the flashlight up to Shiloh's eyes.
   b. He asked Marty if it was Judd Travers' dog.
   c. He told Marty to put the gunnysacks in the jeep.
   d. He carried Shiloh down the hill.
   e. Marty cried without making a sound.
   f. He begged his dad not to take Shiloh back to Judd.
   g. Mr. Preston drove them to Doc Murphy's.
2. a. Doc Murphy examined the wounds.
   b. He gave Shiloh a shot to ease the pain.
   c. He washed the wounds, dressed them and stitched them back up.
   d. He said he can keep Shiloh for a day or two.
3. a. Marty and his dad don't say a word till they get home.
   b. Mr. Preston asks Marty if he has any other secrets.
   c. Marty asks if they can keep Shiloh until he's better.
   d. Marty promises to pay Doc Murphy's bill.
   e. Mr. Preston agrees to keep Shiloh just until he's well.

Pages 37-39 F

1. Summaries will vary.
   The Prestons took Shiloh to Doc Murphy who takes care of him. Marty told his dad he would pay the bill. His dad told him he could keep Shiloh until he is well.
2. a. Marty's dad told Marty he couldn't keep the dog. It belonged to Judd.
   b. Mr. Preston took Shiloh to Doc Murphy.
3. Answers may vary.
   - He was awakened from his sleep, but never complained about it.
   - He said he wasn't a vet, but took care of Shiloh anyway.

4. a. Marty told Doc who owned the dog.
    b. Students need 1 of these answers.
        - Doc sucked in his breath and then let it out a little at a time.
        - Doc said, "Whew!"
5. a. - Marty had to leave Shiloh at Doc's office.
        - Marty had to crawl into the Jeep with his dad afterward.
    b. Answers may vary.
        - He wanted to stay with Shiloh.
        - He knew he was in trouble.
6. Yes, his dad lost trust in Marty. Students need 2 of these answers.
    - He asked Marty what else he didn't know.
    - He asked Marty what else he was keeping from him.
    - After Marty replied, "Nothing!" he asked how he knew that's not another lie.
    - When Marty said it's not a lie, his dad told Marty saying so doesn't make it true.
7. They both cared about how animals are treated.
    Students need 2 of the answers for each person below.
    Mr. Preston
    - Mr. Preston said Marty must do what's right.
    - He believed that the law must be followed.
    - He believed if you don't like a law, then you worked to change it.
    - He said Marty should open his eyes and see the mistreated dogs all around.
    - He said suddenly a dog pulled at Marty's heart and he wants to change things.

Marty
- Marty believed no animal should be left with someone who mistreats and hurts it.
- He asked what his dad would have thought of him if he just left Shiloh for Judd to find and beat.
- He believed that sometimes you don't have time to wait for a law to change.
- He said for things to change, there had to be a first time things are done differently.
8. Students need both answers.
    - Marty could keep Shiloh until he is well.
    - When Shiloh has recovered, they will take him back to Judd.

Chapter 11

Page 40 A

Word	Part of Speech
a. yank	verb
b. antibiotics	noun
c. enthusiasm	noun
d. chugging	verb
e. pesterin'	verb
f. generous	adjective
g. zigzagging	verb
h. warble	verb

Page 41 B

1. helping
2. boredom
3. stopping
4. push
5. hide
6. noiseless
7. selfish
8. germicide

Pages 41-43 C

1. Students need 1 of these answers.
   - He caused his parents to argue.
   - He'd lied and kept secrets from both parents, now they wouldn't trust him.
   - He had Ma keep a secret from Dad, so Dad may not trust Mom anymore.
   - Judd may hold bad feelings for Dad because Marty had his dog.

2. - Becky found out Shiloh was hurt and wanted to know where he was.
   - Dara Lynn was nice to Marty and agreed with his actions.
   - She wished he'd told her about keeping Shiloh.

3. a. - He wished David hadn't come.
      - He wanted to be alone with his feelings.
      - He didn't want to talk to anybody but Doc Murphy.
   b. They:
      - Fly a kite.
      - Chase a groundhog.

4. Wording will vary.
   Marty was trying to keep David from finding Shiloh's pen by suggesting they go eat.

5. Students need 4 answers for each boy.
   David:
   - David looked 'bug-eyed', eyes wide open.
   - He wanted to know what had happened there.
   - David promised not to tell.
   - His eyes were about to pop out of his head.
   - He kept guessing at what had happened.
   - When he heard the story, his mouth fell open.
   - He said, "Wow!"

   Marty:
   - Marty made David sit down and listen.
   - He told David something terrible had happened there.
   - He made David promise to keep it secret.
   - He told about Shiloh and how he was hurt.
   - He said Doc Murphy said they'd know that night how Shiloh was doing.

6. They went into the pen and cleaned up the blood.
   Students need 1 of these answers.
   - Cleaning up was easier with David's help.
   - He believed that he and David would be friends for life.

7. a. Doc Murphy brought Shiloh home.
   b. He meant that he thought it was important to keep Judd from hearing about Shiloh.

8. a. These 3 steps must be in order.
      - Doc should send the bill to Mr. Preston.
      - Mr. Preston would pay it.
      - Marty would pay his dad back.
   b. Doc Murphy said it was a generous thing for Marty to do when it wasn't even his dog.

9. Answers will vary. Possible answers are:
   - Shiloh will be kept in the house.
   - Everybody will take good care of him.

Chapter 12

Page 44 A

Word	Part of Speech
a. slurp	verb
b. squats	verb
c. quavery	adjective
d. sympathy	noun
e. decency	noun
f. figuring	verb
g. turpentine	noun

Page 45 B

1. turpentine
2. sympathy
3. figuring
4. squats
5. slurp
6. quavery
7. decency

Pages 45-47 C

1. Answers will vary.
2. a. Students need 2 of these answers.
   - Around Shiloh, Mr. Preston didn't say much.
   - He stood off to the side.
   - He didn't let Shiloh lick him.
   b. He sees his dad letting Shiloh lick his plate and scratching his back.
3. Wording of answer may vary.
   a. By the time Shiloh is healed, everyone will love him, so they won't let him be returned to Judd.
   b. Students need 1 answer.
   - They didn't have the money to pay Judd
   - There's no money to keep a pet.
4. The family didn't want to get too attached to Shiloh because when he gets well, they know he'd go back to Judd.
   They were waiting for the day that happens.
5. Answers will vary.
   - Everyone pays attention to Shiloh.
   - The parents never say Shiloh's name out loud.
   - Shiloh is getting stronger.
   - He goes outside on his own.
   - Marty continues to look for cans and a job.
6. a. Somebody would tell Judd where his dog is.
   b. Students need 3 steps in order.
   - A patient of Doc Murphy saw a beagle on Doc's porch.
   - The patient told Judd he thought it might be his.
   - Judd went to see the dog at Doc's.
   - Doc told him who brought Shiloh in and where he was.
7. Students need 3 of these answers.
   - Judd said the Prestons have his dog, but they didn't have the decency to tell him.
   - When he saw how hurt Shiloh was, he yelled, "Look what you done to my dog!"
   - Judd said he'd never caused a dog an injury like that.
   - He said it wouldn't have happened if they'd brought the dog back to him like he told them.
8. a. Ma asked Judd how much he wants for the dog, so The Prestons can buy it.
   b. • Judd said the dog's not for sale.
   - Since it was them paying to fix him up, he'd let them keep him until Sunday.

Chapter 13

Page 48 A

Word	Part of Speech
a. rehearsed	verb
b. investigator	noun
c. padlocked	verb
d. quarrel	noun
e. scale	verb
f. allergic	adjective

Page 49 B
Answers will vary.

Page 49-51 C
1. Wording of answers may vary.
   a. Dad-Sometimes it's hard but you have to do what has to be done.
   b. Ma- At least Marty brought some joy and kindness to Shiloh and Shiloh will never forget Marty.
   c. David- His aunt and uncle can't take Shiloh because his aunt is allergic to dogs.
2. a. Marty thought he could hide Shiloh at the old gristmill.
   b. Students need 1 of these answers.
      - He couldn't take Shiloh out except after dark.
      - It would be no life for a dog.
      - Judd lived close by and the other dogs might sniff him out.
3. a. Ma and the girls loved and trusted Shiloh.
   b. Students need both these answers.
      - "If Becky ever fell in the creek, I'll bet Shiloh'd pull her out."
      - "If I ever saw a snake, I'll bet Shiloh'd kill it for me."
4. a. Marty was walking to Judd Travers' place.
   b. He was going to tell Judd he was not going to give Shiloh back.
5. a. Marty was going to offer to buy Shiloh.
   b. Answers will vary. Possible answers:
      - If Judd refused to sell him, Marty would take Shiloh away.
      - Judd would have to take Marty to court to get Shiloh back.
      - Marty would tell the judge how Judd treats his animals.
6. Students need 4 of these answers.
   - Marty could get his dad in a lot of trouble.
   - It's serious when a quarrel with a neighbor goes to the law.
   - If it comes to taking a man's property, he figures folks will side with Judd.
   - He's not making life easier for his family.
   - He won't give Shiloh up without a fight.
   - Judd might shoot Marty.
7. Wording will vary.
   a. He sees a rabbit and a doe.
   b. • The rabbit runs in front of him.
      - It hides in some bushes.
      - The female deer is munching in the meadow. Judd kills her.

Chapter 14

Page 52 A

Word	Part of Speech
a. slogs	verb
b. intention	noun
c. regulation	adjective
d. camouflage	adjective

Page 52 B
1. slogs
2. camouflage
3. regulation
4. intention

Pages 53-55 C
1. a. Students need 1 of these answers.
   - happy
   - delighted
   - joyful

   b. Students need 1 of these answers.
   - He has a weird grin on his face.
   - He says "Whoeee" "I got 'er!"

   c. Students need 1 of these answers.
   - surprised
   - startled

   d. Students need 1 of these answers.
   - He whirls around and sees Marty.
   - He asks "Where'd you come from?"

2. Student answers will vary.
   - He felt like he had some power over Judd.
   - He'd caught Judd breaking the law.
   - He'd never kill an animal, especially out of season.
   - He felt superior to Judd.
   - He could report Judd to the game warden.

3. a. It wasn't deer hunting season.
   b. He would be fined $200 for killing a doe out of season.
   c. The does have fawns (baby deer) which keeps the species going. OR: The doe could have had a baby that would now starve to death.

4. a. Answers will vary.
   b. If Yes, the 'why' might be:
   - Marty had caught him doing something wrong.
   - He was afraid Marty would get him in trouble. If No, the 'why not' might be:
   - He was angry with himself for getting caught.

5. a. Students need 3 of these answers:
   - He told Judd, "That's a lie."
   - He said deer aren't in season and there's a fine for killing one.
   - He told Judd, "Yeah. I'll tell (the game warden)."
   - He said he'd get the game warden there to see evidence of the killing. Then find the deer at Judd's.
   - He asked Judd if he was going to shoot him like that dog he found 6 months ago with a bullet in its head.
   - He told Judd if people find him dead, his dad will know whose bullet killed him.

   b. Anything along these lines is acceptable.
   - Marty spoke that way to Judd because he knew he could make trouble for Judd.
   - He wasn't afraid of Judd.
   - He was thinking of getting to keep Shiloh.

6. a. Judd would give Marty half of the deer meat if he didn't tell.
   b. Marty wanted Shiloh.

7. - Marty would work for Judd for $2.00 an hour for 20 hours to pay the $40.00 Judd wanted for Shiloh.

- Marty got Shiloh.
8. a. He was getting Shiloh.
   b. He was putting other deer in danger by not reporting Judd.
9. Marty wanted Judd to put it in writing.
10. • After the evidence (the deer) is gone, Judd won't give Shiloh to Marty..
    • Judd will say he never wrote on the grocery sack; that Marty wrote it himself.
    • Marty's biggest worry is that someday Judd will see Shiloh running in the woods and shoot him.

Chapter 15

Page 56 A

Across
3. jubilation
6. legal
7. sift
8. afford
11. wedge

Down
1. whetstone
2. kindling
4. locust
5. rarin'
7. scooting
9. definite
10. squaller

Pages 57-58 B
Sentences will vary. Part of Speech:
1. adjective
2. verb
3. verb
4. noun
5. verb
6. noun
7. verb
8. noun/noun
9. adjective
10. noun
11. noun

Page 59 C
1. legal
2. afford
3. squaller
4. jubilation
5. rarin'
6. sift
7. locust
8. kindling
9. definite
10. wedge
11. scooting
12. whetstone

Pages 59-60 D

Marty - Figured out how to explain things without lying; decided to work for Shiloh rather than hide him or lie about him; first hated Judd more than the devil, then felt a fraction of an ounce of sorry for Judd because he didn't have a father who did things with him.

Judd- Began talking with Marty about dogs and hunting; put cold water out for him; gave him a collar for Shiloh.

Mr. Preston - Agreed the family can keep Shiloh; was proud of Marty, not upset with him.

Shiloh - Was finally learning to bark, to make a sound.

Pages 60-63 E
1. • Marty's dad didn't quite believe it; he seemed suspicious.
   • His mom is happy; she figures Judd didn't want a lame dog.
2. Wording of answers may vary.
   a. Marty had to decide whether:
      • To lie by omission to his parents and not tell about the deer.
      • To tell the whole truth and have lied to Judd in promising

       not to tell about the deer.

    b. • Lying by omission means to only tell part of the truth, usually the part that won't make things worse.

3. Answers may vary along the content below.

  Mr. Preston meant that they would nourish Shiloh's body with food and Shiloh would nourish their spirits with happiness and love. Shiloh would make them feel good inside. He made it sound like a good trade.

4. a. Marty howled with joy and Shiloh joined in.

    b. Shiloh had never made a sound without being punished, so he had to learn how to bark. His first try wasn't very strong.

5. • Marty figured Judd wanted him to do a bad job so Judd could get Shiloh back.

  • He was trying to break Marty's back or spirit or both, so Marty would quit working and Judd could get Shiloh back.

6. Students need 2 of these answers.
- Judd talked about kicking his dogs.
- He bragged that he never beat them with a stick.
- He threw his Pabst can at the dogs.
- He yelled at them.

7. Students need 10 of these answers in order.

Judd asked Marty to:
- Carry the deer.
- Stack the woodpile.
- Re-stack it according to size.
- Hoe the dirt between the corn.
- Scrub the sides of his trailer and porch.
- Shine the windows.
- Rake the yard.
- Pick beans.
- Split wood.
- Dig a ditch for garbage.
- Hoe the cornfield again.
- Scrub the porch.
- Weed the bean patch.

8. a. Judd said:
- That Marty was putting in a lot of work for nothing.
- That their written agreement wasn't legal because there were no witnesses.

    b. Students need 1 of these answers.
- Marty kept working because he wants Shiloh.
- Marty was going to keep his end of the bargain.
- Marty felt the hard work would be worth it when Shiloh belonged to him.

    c. Students must have this answer.
- Marty told Judd that they made a bargain and he aims to keep his part of it.

9. a. • Marty uses the sickle to cut the tall grass.
- He sharpens the sickle with a whetstone.

    b. Judd pretends to be asleep to see if Marty will quit before his two hours is up.

10. Even though Judd told him he's not paying one cent more, Marty kept on working past his time.

11. Students need 1 of these answers.
- Marty decided he had no choice except to stick to his side of the deal, because if he quit, he knew Judd would come for Shiloh.
- Marty didn't want to make Judd mad, because if Shiloh were running loose, Judd might kill him.

12. a. Marty asks Judd how he got interested in hunting. Judd tells him about hunting a few times with his dad when he was little, and that it was the only nice thing he remembered about him.

   b. Marty feels a little sorry for him, especially when he thinks on all the things he'd done with his own dad.

13. Students need 2 of these answers.
   - Because somehow Judd and Marty had learned to get along.
   - Judd, in his way, was showing Marty he had no hard feelings toward him.
   - Judd was showing that he respected the fact that Marty kept up his end of the bargain.
   - Judd may be trying to apologize for overworking Marty by giving him a "bonus."